Carlo Goldoni: A Servant to Two Masters
a new adaptation by Lee Hall

A co-production between the Young Vic Theatre Company and the RSC, *A Servant to Two Masters* was first performed at The Other Place, Stratford-upon-Avon, in December 1999, and at the Young Vic in January 2000.

Carlo Goldoni (1707–93) was an Italian dramatist born in Venice. His many popular comedies include *A Servant to Two Masters (Il Servitore di due Padroni)* (1746), *The Respectable Woman (La Putta Onorata)* (1749) and *The Mistress of the Inn (La Locandieva)* (1753). In 1762 Goldoni moved to Paris where he directed the Italian theatre and continued to write more plays, including *The Fan (Il Ventaglio)* (1764). During his lifetime Goldoni wrote over 200 comedies, tragedies and tragicomedies and reformed the Italian stage.

Lee Hall's theatre work includes translations of Buchner's *Leonce and Lena* (Gate Theatre), Brecht's *Mr Puntilla and his Man Matti* (The Right Size/Almeida, Traverse and West End), and *Mother Courage and her Children* (Shared Experience). His adaptation of his award-winning radio play *Spoonface Steinberg* will be produced at the Royal National Theatre in January 2000 and a new stage play *Cooking with Elvis* (Edinburgh Festival 1999) opens in the West End. Lee is currently filming *Dancer*, directed by Stephen Daldry, and will shortly be filming an adaptation of his prize-winning radio play *I Love You Jimmy Spud*. His television work includes *Ted and Alice*, *The Student Prince* and *Spoonface Steinberg*.

D1110438

also available

Cooking with Elvis & Bollocks
Spoonface Steinberg

A Servant to Two Masters

by
Carlo Goldoni

a new adaptation by
Lee Hall

from a literal translation by
Gwenda Pandolfi

Published by Methuen 1999

1 3 5 7 9 10 8 6 4 2

First published in the United Kingdom in 1999 by
Methuen Publishing Limited
215 Vauxhall Bridge Road
London, SW1V 1EJ

Peribo Pty Ltd, 58 Beaumont Road, Mount Kuring-Gai
NSW 2080, Australia, ACN 002 273 761

Copyright © 1999 Lee Hall

The right of Lee Hall to be identified as the author of this work has been
asserted by him in accordance with the Copyright, Designs and Patents
Act, 1988

Methuen Publishing Limited
Reg. No. 3543167

A CIP catalogue record for this book is available from the British Library

ISBN 0 413 74850 2

Typeset by SX Composing DTP, Rayleigh, Essex
Printed and bound in Great Britain by
Cox & Wyman Ltd, Reading, Berkshire

Caution
All rights in this play are strictly reserved and application
for performance, etc. should be made before rehearsals begin to Rod Hall,
The Rod Hall Agency Ltd, 7 Goodge Place, London W1P 1FL. No
performance may be given unless a licence has been obtained.

This book is sold subject to the condition that it shall not, by way of trade
or otherwise, be lent, resold, hired out, or otherwise circulated in any other
form of binding or cover than that in which it is published and without a
similar condition, including this condition, being imposed on the
subsequent purchaser.

THE ROYAL SHAKESPEARE COMPANY

The Royal Shakespeare Company is probably one of the best-known theatre companies in the world. It has operated in its present form since 1961 when, under the leadership of the young Peter Hall, it changed its name from the Shakespeare Memorial Theatre Company, established a London base and widened its repertoire to embrace works other than Shakespeare.

Today the RSC has five home theatres. In Stratford the Royal Shakespeare Theatre stages large-scale productions of Shakespeare's plays; the Swan, a galleried Jacobean playhouse, brings to light the plays of many of his neglected contemporaries alongside classics of world theatre, while The Other Place, the company's studio theatre, houses some of the company's most exciting experimental and contemporary work, as well as providing a regular venue for visiting companies and some of the RSC's education work, including the annual Prince of Wales Shakespeare School.

In 1982 the company moved its London home to the Barbican Centre, where in the large-scale Barbican Theatre and the studio-sized Pit, the company stages productions transferring from Stratford as well as new productions.

But Stratford and London are only part of the story. Recent years have seen a dramatic increase in the reach of the RSC, with major RSC productions on tour around the UK and abroad, in addition to the company's annual resident seasons in Newcastle upon Tyne and Plymouth. Productions from Stratford and London visit regional theatres, while our annual regional tour continues to set up its own travelling auditorium in schools and community centres around the country. This ensures that the RSC's productions are available to the widest possible number of people geographically. A lively education programme accompanies all this work, creating the audiences of tomorrow by bringing the excitement and the power of theatre to young people all over the country.

Outside the UK, the support of Allied Domecq, whose principal sponsorship of the RSC from 1994 to 2001 reached a record-breaking £7.7 million - the UK's largest single arts sponsorship - has, amongst other activities, enabled the RSC to undertake a regular international touring programme. In the past few years the company has taken Shakespeare to enthusiastic audiences in Europe, the USA, Australia, New Zealand, South America, Japan, India and Pakistan. In 2000, the company will visit Hong Kong, Spain, Turkey and Korea. The RSC is grateful to The British Council for its support of its overseas touring programme.

Despite the RSC's growth from Stratford festival theatre to international status, the company is still formed around a core of associate actors and actresses, whose artistic talents combine with those of the world's top directors and designers and the most highly-skilled technical workshops to give a distinctive and unmistakable approach to theatre. The play you are seeing tonight is at once a link in a great tradition and a unique event.

THE OTHER PLACE

The Other Place is the RSC's smallest theatre, where you may have seen productions as diverse as *Henry VI*, *The Learned Ladies*, *Pentecost* and *Oroonoko*. The theatre also houses our rehearsal studios and has a central role in the history of the RSC as a centre for research and development.

Our roots lie in two distinct areas. In the early 1960s Michel St Denis brought to the company the European tradition of 'the actors' laboratory' and worked with actors, directors, writers, designers and technical staff to develop, singly and together, their own craft and imagination and that of the company.

While the company continued to explore ways of revealing Elizabethan drama, actors and directors sought new audiences for new work. Theatregoround was born. This was the first small-scale work the company had done and it laid the foundation for subsequent seasons at The Roundhouse and The Place in London. The 'tin hut' became The Other Place and Buzz Goodbody its first artistic director.

In the present-day TOP we remember Buzz Goodbody and Michel St Denis in the rehearsal rooms named after them, and their legacy continues in our developmental work. Each year we work with actors to assemble a programme of workshops focusing on different disciplines. We are members of the Union of European Theatres and each year RSC actors, directors and designers meet their European counterparts for an exchange of ideas. Members of our local community visit The Other Place for a variety of reasons: last year students from the local college performed a season of work, primary school children and under-fives join poetry performances and workshops, and our café area houses changing exhibitions by local and national artists.

Over the years, The Other Place has produced work by most of the major contemporary dramatists – David Rudkin, Mike Leigh, Willy Russell, Edward Bond, Howard Brenton, Nick Dear, and more recently, Peter Whelan, Pam Gems, Robert Holman, Derek Walcott, David Edgar, April de Angelis, 'Biyi Bandele and Bernard-Marie Koltes. Alongside these the classical balance has been maintained with new productions of European classics and Shakespeare. As well as new plays in performance, we run workshops with young writers, giving them the chance to work with RSC actors on themes which reflect the concerns of the classical repertoire.

Our public work continues the theme of exploration and innovation and we are very pleased to renew our relationship with the Young Vic in this co-production of *A Servant To Two Masters*. Our previous co-productions were *Beckett Shorts* (in partnership with four European theatres) and *The Dispute* (with the Lyric Theatre, Hammersmith), which won two TMA awards.

Steven Pimlott,
Director, The Other Place.

RSC EDUCATION

The RSC runs a substantial education programme, reaching people through workshops, projects and publications: a new Director has been appointed to expand the RSC's work in these fields and to build a creative new technology programme. There is a full schedule of training opportunities for teachers, from practical workshops to short courses, focusing on Shakespeare and the theatre arts. For a teachers' brochure, please call 01789 403462. RSC Education also contributes to the company's programme of pre- and post-show events based on the repertoire.

The RSC Education web-site address is www.rsc.org.uk/education.
To keep up to date with the programme and new projects, join the Education mailing list. Details from the RSC Membership Office on 01789 403440.

Other events throughout the season
Pre-performance and after-show events which complement the repertoire and put the RSC's work in context. These are scheduled in the main RSC leaflet and in programmes. Tickets can be booked through the Box Office.

Talkback
An opportunity for audiences to respond immediately to the performance they have just seen and to discuss the production with members of the acting company. Talkback events are free and are scheduled in the RSC leaflet and nightly programmes.

JOIN THE RSC

For £8 a year you can join the **RSC's Mailing List** as an Associate member. Regular mailings will bring you:

* **Advance information and priority booking** for all RSC seasons in Stratford, London, Newcastle and Plymouth

* **Deferred payment facilities** for the London Season and the Stratford Summer Festival Season 2000 when tickets are paid for by credit card

* **Seasonal offers on the Stratford StopOver scheme**

* **Special members' events** in Stratford and London

* **Details of UK and overseas touring** and information about RSC transfers to the **West End**

* **Free RSC Magazine**

* **No fees payable on ticket re-sales** in Stratford

Full membership at £24, **social groups** at £10 and **education groups** at £8 give even more benefits.

Overseas Members Wherever you are in the world, you can be a member of the RSC's Mailing List. Overseas Membership is available from £15.

For further information, please write to the Membership Office, Royal Shakespeare Theatre, Stratford-upon-Avon, CV37 6BB, or telephone (01789) 403440

STAY IN TOUCH

For up-to-date news on the RSC, our productions and education work, visit the RSC's official web site: **www.rsc.org.uk**. Further information on the RSC is also available on Teletext.

on Ch4 p450

A PARTNERSHIP WITH THE RSC

The RSC sets standards everywhere we go and in everything we do.

The RSC sells well over 1 million tickets each year.

The RSC performs over 30 productions each year.

The RSC plays more than 260 weeks of performances each year.

The RSC turnover exceeds £30 million each year.

The RSC visits more than 30 UK towns and cities each year.

The RSC undertakes 50 or more weeks of touring in the UK and overseas each year.

The RSC works with over 500 educational establishments each year.

The RSC Development Department raises more than £6 million from sponsorship and fundraising programmes each year.

The RSC employs over 750 people.

The RSC generates more than 60% of its annual income from ticket sales and commercial activities.

The RSC generates expenditure of almost £34 million for the West Midlands, supporting 250 companies and over 1,000 jobs.

The RSC is recognised as being the most cost-efficient organisation of its kind in the UK and 'an exceptionally well run organisation'.
(Arts Council Appraisal)

Behind these figures is an exciting array of partnership opportunities for companies and individuals. The RSC raises nearly £2 million in corporate sponsorship each year, and even greater sums are raised from charitable trusts, foundations and individual donations. This enables the RSC to undertake initiatives such as actor training, education workshops and improving disabled access, and helps to maintain the highest standards in everything we do.

The RSC is grateful for the valuable support of all its sponsors and supporters during the season. We particularly thank Allied Domecq, principal sponsor since 1994, for their far-sighted and long-standing relationship. Allied Domecq's announcement that their principal sponsorship will be coming to a natural end in 2001 provides an exciting opportunity for companies to form new corporate partnerships with the RSC, and to utilise the expertise the RSC has gained in the commercial sector.

For further information on corporate or individual partnerships with the RSC, please contact :
Jonathan Pope, Development Director,
Royal Shakespeare Company, Waterside, Stratford-upon-Avon, Warwickshire,
CV37 6BB. Tel. 01789 412603.

www.rsc.org.uk/development

ALLIED DOMECQ
Principal Sponsor of the RSC

THE SPONSORS CLUB
Newcastle Season: Allied Domecq, Barclays, Benfield Motors Group,
Fenwick, Maersk Air, Northern Electric & Gas, Northern Rock, Northern
Venture Managers*, Northumbrian Water Group, Origin*, Procter & Gamble,
University of Northumbria, VA TECH Reyrolle*

RSC South West Sponsors
Plymouth Season: Allied Domecq, Pennon Group plc, First Great Western,
Plymouth College of Further Education, SWEB, Carlton

PRODUCTION SPONSORS
BIG STEAK PUB *Antony and Cleopatra*

WACKY WAREHOUSE *The Lion, the Witch and the Wardrobe*

BALLANTINE'S *King Lear*

LAPHROAIG *Volpone*

JBA *The Family Reunion*

LAPHROAIG *Tales From Ovid*

PLATINUM CORPORATE MEMBERS *Oroonoko*

Don Carlos is supported by RSC PATRONS

PERFORMANCE SPONSORS
Origin*, Jaguar Cars Limited, Cheltenham & Gloucester, Honeywell,
Schroders

1999 LORD MAYORS GALA Schroders

THE ROYAL SHAKESPEARE THEATRE TRUST
The RSC is particularly grateful for the continuing support of the Royal
Shakespeare Theatre Trust. An independently registered charity, the Trust's
prime objective is to raise funds to support the entire range of the RSC's
activities within the UK and abroad.

The RSC is grateful to The British Council for its support of its overseas
touring programme.

CORPORATE MEMBERS
Platinum Members
Bacon & Woodrow, Clifford Chance, Marks & Spencer, Origin UK Limited

Gold Members
The British Land Company plc, Eversheds, KPMG, Linklaters, Moore
Stephens, The National Grid Company plc, PowerGen UK plc, Reuters,
Rover Group, Severn Trent plc, Transco, The Ulanov Partnership*

Silver Members
Arthur Andersen, Barclays Bank plc, Brewin Dolphin Holdings plc*,
British Gas, Brown, Shipley & Co. Ltd., Great Malvern Holdings Limited,
Grove Industries Limited, Kerry Ingredients, Knight Frank, Lazard Brothers
& Co., Limited, Lex Service plc, McFadden, Pilkington & Ward, Pettifer Ltd,
Rowe & Maw, Standard Chartered Bank, Titmuss Sainer Dechert,
Tomkins plc, Warner Cranston Solicitors, Weirgrove Automation Ltd.

The RSC is also grateful for the following sponsorships:

TRANSCO

CARLTON
Stratford Theatre Tours

Sponsorship in kind
JAGUAR CARS, LDV, MAERSK AIR, TRUCKLINE FERRIES

DONATIONS
The RSC is grateful for recent generous donations from the following trusts,
foundations and individuals. Our thanks also to the substantial number of
people who have contributed to our work, but who we are unable to list here.

Anon
Mr Neville Abraham, Mr and Mrs Jamil Amyuni, Mr and Mrs Peter Beckwith,
Mr David Beresford Jones, Mr Robert Bourne and Miss Sally Greene,
Mr and Mrs Bruce Burgess, Mr and Mrs Ronnie Cohen, Mr Gavyn Davies,
Dr Gert-Rudolf Flick, Foster Charitable Trust, Miss Sara Galbraith and
Mr Robert Ham QC, The Gatsby Charitable Foundation, Grand Charity of
Freemasons, Mrs Drue Heinz DBE, The Alan Edward Higgs Charity,
Ms Annette Holm and Mr Bertil Nygren, Mr and Mrs Greg Hutchings,
Mr and Mrs Alton Irby III, Mr Laurence Isaacson CBE, Mr Alan Jones OBE, Mr
Donald Kahn, Sir Eddie Kulukundis OBE, Mr Elias Kulukundis,
Mr and Mrs Stathes Kulukundis, The Joicey Trust, Mr and Mrs Ian Laing,
The Laura Pels Foundation, The Henphil Pillsbury Fund of the Minneapolis
Foundation, The Sir Cyril Kleinwort Charitable Settlement,
Mr David Martinez, Mr John McLaren, Mr and Mrs Michael Neal,
The Niarchos Foundation, The Hon Mr and Mrs Christopher Portman,
Mr and Mrs John Ritblat, CA Rookes Charitable Trust, The Said Foundation,
Schroder Charity Trust, The Ratcliff Foundation, Mr and Mrs John Thornton,
Baron and Baroness Thyssen-Bornemisza de Kaszon, Mr and Mrs Alfred
Vinton, Mr and Mrs Adrian Watney, Mr Nigel Weiss, Mr Shaun Woodward MP

In memory of;
Mrs Lorna Hughes, Gladys Beatrice Whittingham

Arts Council of England Lottery Fund

RSC PATRONS
RSC Patrons continue a tradition of private patronage that dates back to
Shakespeare's day. The support of RSC Patrons enables the RSC to sustain
its artistic achievement and keep Shakespeare's work available and
affordable to all.

The RSC is grateful to RSC Patrons for their support of this season's
production of *Don Carlos*

Patrons
Anon
David and Elizabeth Acland, Lord Alexander of Weedon*,
Dr and Mrs WEK Anderson*, Neil Benson, David and Sandra Burbidge,
The Hon Rupert Carington*, Lady Cass*, Mr and Mrs Robert Craig,
Mrs Felicia Crystal*, Gavyn Davies, Glen and Deborah Davis,
Sir William Dugdale, Ray and Eileen Dunn*, Robyn Durie*, Jane M and
Howard D Epstein*, Mr and Mrs James Evans*, Liam Fisher-Jones*,
Sir Christopher Foster, Sally Greene, Charlotte Heber Percy, Mrs Drue Heinz
DBE*, Dr Thomas Jensen*, Sir Eddie Kulukundis OBE*, Mr & Mrs Ian Laing,
Joan and Philip Livesey, Mr and Mrs Brian McGowan, Mr and Mrs Conrad
Meyer III*, Dr Barbara Oldham*, Lord Palumbo*, Mr and Mrs Philip
Pillsbury*, Jonathan Pope, His Honour Judge Michael Rich QC*,
Catherine Roe, Ian Rushton, Lord and Lady Sainsbury of Turville*,
Mr & Mrs Albert Scardino, Mr and Mrs Steven Scheuer, Donald R Seawell*,
Mr and Mrs Andrew Seth*, F William Shea, Mr and Mrs Alan Shelley*, Denis
Shorrock, Michael and Julie Simmons, Mr David Tang OBE*,
Mr T L Ward, Colin and Mary Wells, Professor Stanley Wells*, William
Weston, Patricia Whitehead*, Dr John Wollaston, *Denotes Founder Patron

To recognise and thank RSC Patrons for their donations, the RSC offers
different levels of involvement encompassing all RSC performances in
Stratford, London, Newcastle, Plymouth and overseas.

Arts & Business
PAIRING SCHEME

NVM, VA TECH Reyrolle, Origin, The Ulanov Partnership and Brewin Dolphin Holdings plc are award winners under the
Arts & Business Pairing Scheme for their support of the RSC. Arts & Business is funded by the Arts Council of England and
the Department of Culture, Media and Sport.

YOUNG VIC

The Young Vic Theatre Company brings new versions of classic stories and great plays to audiences of all ages and backgrounds. Committed to making theatre available to all, particularly the young, we cultivate new audiences and integrate our productions with extensive off-stage work with partners in education and the community.

Teaching others about theatre, and learning ourselves from this activity, is integral to the Young Vic. We provide young people with the practical means to explore theatre through the skills and experience of our award-winning core creative team.

In recognition of our national and international reputation, we take our work beyond this theatre to audiences throughout Britain and across the world. We invite other leading theatre companies, who share our approaches to theatre, to bring their work to audiences at the Young Vic.

THE YOUNG VIC THEATRES

Main House

The main auditorium at the Young Vic is one of London's most adaptable spaces. It is used to great effect to house a wide range of new works by outstanding artists, from magical adaptations of stories such as *Arabian Nights* and *Grimm Tales* to uncompromising new versions of Genet and Shakespeare.

The performance arenas of Ancient Greece and Rome originally inspired its design, seating up to 500 people. Performances are given in-the-round, thrust, traverse or in fact any number of variations, and the unique nature of the auditorium means that the audience is never far from the stage, able to enjoy a great view of the action.

To allow us to use the main auditorium as flexibly as possible, we have unreserved seating which lets us position the audience in the best possible relationship to the stage area. We do not actually confirm our maximum seating capacity until the first preview performance, thus further enabling the seating configuration to be adapted in direct response to developments in on-stage rehearsals. We could not introduce reserved seating and maintain this distinctive flexibility of the auditorium, and we hope that each time you enter the Young Vic Theatre you are pleasantly surprised by our inventive set designs and stage configurations.

Young Vic Studio

The Young Vic Studio is one of London's most important homes of experimental new theatre. Leading companies present work that subverts, questions and reflects contemporary life. Seating up to 80 people, and first used for performances in 1984, it is similarly flexible in configuration to the main auditorium. If you come and see a show in the Studio theatre you could find yourself sitting in-the-round, along one side, in the middle or even walking about as the performance takes place around you.

GET INVOLVED – TEACHING, PARTICIPATION AND RESEARCH

From doing workshops with actors and directors to attending performances for free or even working on your own production, the Young Vic Theatre Company offers a range of ways to get involved in theatre and support our work.

We provide young people from 3 to 20 years old with the practical means to explore theatre through the skills and experience of our award-winning core creative team. This process of research directly informs our work on stage.

Our programme includes: theatre-making activities; music, text, voice and body teaching projects; on-stage production workshops; a Schools' Theatre Festival; written resource material; workshops with both studio practitioners and young professionals and an extensive work experience and apprenticeship programme.

All the work is free of charge to participants and runs in tandem with the Funded Ticket Scheme that offers access to performances through free or highly subsidised tickets. Currently our activities primarily focus on the London inner city boroughs of Lambeth and Southwark with the expectation of developing links with other South East London Boroughs.For more information please write to us: TPR, Young Vic, 66 The Cut, London SE1 8LZ

AUDIENCE DEVELOPMENT – THE YOUNG VIC FUNDED TICKET SCHEME

The Young Vic Funded Ticket Scheme (main sponsor Allied Domecq plc) provides an introduction to theatre for thousands of people from all social and economic backgrounds who might not have considered a trip to see live theatre. Initially created in 1994 to enable local school children, based on need, to visit the theatre for the first time, the scheme has been radically expanded owing to a successful application to the National Lottery's Arts for Everyone programme.

The expanded Funded Ticket Scheme, now in its second year, brought close to 10,000 new theatregoers to the Young Vic during year one. If you would like further information on how a group from your place of work or organisation within London or the home counties can become involved, please call the Audience Development Department on 0207 633 0133.

YOUNG VIC – FUNDING AND INCOME

The Young Vic receives annual funding from the Arts Council of England, London Arts Board, London Borough Grants and Lambeth and Southwark Councils. These grants represent 37% of annual income. A further 4% is realised through Fund Raising and Donations. The remaining 59% of annual income is generated through the Box Office, theatre hires, programme sales etc.

In the last 12 months over 80,000 people have attended performances at the Young Vic, we have worked with over 7,000 young people in London's inner-city communities and over 10,000 have experienced the magic of live theatre (many for the first time) through our Funded Ticket Scheme.

The Young Vic's annual programme of work, including 5 productions annually, national and international touring, theatre workshops, the Funded Ticket Scheme, building maintenance, overheads etc, costs approximately £2m. It is with thanks to our funders, sponsors, donors and you the audience that we have been able to develop as a vital and vibrant resource. We look forward to your continued support.

ARTS FOR EVERYONE

In September 1997, the Young Vic was awarded one of the highest National Lottery Arts for Everyone (A4E) awards in the country. This three-year award has enabled us to better resource and realise our core activities, which are crucial to the Young Vic's continued development. Some of these core activities are:

The growth of the Young Vic's Funded Ticket Scheme, which is one of the largest audience development access projects in the country.
The encouragement of young artists on the cutting edge of performance to develop their work through experimentation in the Young Vic's award-winning Studio.
A substantial and significant increase in the Young Vic's acclaimed work with teachers, schools, colleges and young people.
More adequate resources for Young Vic Productions, which has enabled us to bring to the stage outstanding productions by some of Britain's leading talents.

This additional funding will cease in 2001, and we are currently devising strategies to replace this funding and ensure that the artistic and financial success of recent years continues.
In order to realise the enormous potential that this award promises, the Young Vic must find companies, trusts and individuals who share in its commitment to this programme of work. Over the three years of the grant award, the Young Vic must raise a total of £100,000 in partnership funding to release this remarkable lottery award. We take this opportunity to acknowledge the support of Allied Domecq plc in providing a much-needed lead gift of £36,000 over three years, together with the generous support of David and Maria Willetts, The Royal Victoria Hall Foundation, J Sainsbury plc, Direct Connection, 3i Trustee Company Ltd, Shell International Ltd and The McKenna Charitable Trust.

BECOME A PART OF THE FUTURE OF BRITISH THEATRE

If you have enjoyed this performance why not become a Friend of the Young Vic and enjoy a wealth of special Friends' activities and behind-the-scenes glimpses of the varied work of the Young Vic – regarded by many as the future of British Theatre.

Above all, your support will help us to maintain our position as a leading centre for theatre which embraces people of all ages and backgrounds.

The Young Vic takes this opportunity to express its particular thanks to those who have kindly agreed to support our work at the following levels of support:

PATRON
Mr C J Bates
Katie Bradford
Lou Coulson
Ruth Downing
Jeremy Drax
Jennifer Gubbins
Clare Garvin
The Kings School, Canterbury
Dr and Mrs Herzberg
Patrick McKenna
Lady Lever
Dr Martin Smith
Terence Pentony
Jan Topham
Andy Stinson
Val Gilbert Ltd
Diane Sundt
Sybella Zisman
The Tracy Family
Gerry Wade
Robert Hasty
Rebecca Wennington-Ingram

BENEFACTOR
Norma Acland
David Day
Christina Burton
Gillian Diamond
Michael Greenhalgh
Allegra Castellini
R F P Hardman
Sheila Harvey
Jessica Fenton
Lew Hodges
Joanna Howard
Trevor Parsons
Anya Jones
Victoria Neumark Jones
Nick Pizey
Stuart and Julie Maister
Mina Martinez
Anthony Salz
David and Anthea Minnet
Barbara Minto
Richard Slater
Dr Oppenheimer
Mrs G M C Phillips
David Van Oss

C Polemis
Barbara Poole
Anda Winters
Murray Shanks
Mr K H Simmonds
Paula Clement
Mr M Graham-Smith Ann and Peter Snow
Jean Elliott
Janet Walker
Anthony Watkinson
Bruce & Clare Johnson
Mr and Mrs George White
Penny Whitson
Richard Price Television Ltd.
Carmi Weinzweig

Our thanks, too, to our many Friends who have kindly joined at the Supporter and Contributor levels and, of course, our many Young Friends.

For further information on becoming a Friend of the Young Vic please take a leaflet from the display in the foyer or contact the Young Vic Development Office on 0171 633 0133.

The Young Vic would like to express its sincere thanks to the many companies, foundations and private contributors who recognise the value of the company's work. These include:

Abbey National Charitable Trust Limited, Allied Domecq plc, Ambrose and Ann Appelbe Trust, The Avenue Charitable Trust, Barclays Bank plc, Barclays Life Assurance Company Ltd, Bass PLC, Beechdean Dairies Ltd, Thomas Bendhem, The Berkeley Group plc, British Steel plc, Calouste Gulbenkian Foundation, Carlton Television Trust, The Coutts Charitable Trust, David Cohen Family Charitable Trust, The Muriel and Gershon Coren Charitable Foundation, The D'Oyly Carte Charitable Trust, David S Smith Holdings plc, The Eric Evans Memorial Trust, Evening Standard, Frogmore Estates plc, The Robert Gavron Charitable Trust, The Worshipful Company of Grocers, The Guardian Royal Exchange Charitable Trust, Mrs Margaret Guido's Charitable Trust, The Haberdashers' Company, Sue Hammerson's Charitable Trust, Help a London Child, Imperial Chemical Industries plc, The Inverforth Charitable Trust, John Lewis Partnership plc, The Ian Karten Trust, Mathilda and Terence Kennedy Charitable Trust, Konditor & Cook, The Lambert Charitable Trust, Corporation of London, The Lynn Foundation, Manches & Co, Marks and Spencer plc, The Milbourn Charitable Trust, The Peter Minet Trust, Peter Moores Foundation, Newcomen Collett Foundation, PricewaterhouseCoopers, Railtrack plc, The Rayne Foundation, The Reuter Foundation, Royal and Sun Alliance Insurance Group plc, Sir Walter St John's Educational Charity, St Olave's and St Saviour's Grammar School Foundation, Simon's Charity, Singer & Friedlander Limited, Snipe Charitable Trust, South West Trains Limited, The Stanley Foundation Ltd, Sir John Swire CBE and Lady Swire, The Vandervell Foundation, Garfield Weston Foundation, The Whitbread 1988 Charitable Trust, The Harold Hyam Wingate Foundation and our many Friends of the Young Vic

The Young Vic gratefully acknowledges a French Theatre Season Award for research into French Theatre

The Young Vic on the World Wide Web is supported by Direct Connection. The Young Vic is supported by: London Arts Board, the London Borough of Lambeth, London Borough Grants, the London Borough of Southwark, and the National Lottery, issued through the Arts Council of England.

Contents

Introduction

Carlo Goldoni (1707–1793), known as one of the masters of the comic stage, was a failed tragedian. His first works for the stage (although they never actually made it) were in fact tragedies. His first play *Amalasonte – A Lyrical Tragedy* did not, by his own admission, 'make the choice of connoisseurs'. After a few subsequent failures Goldoni pursued a career in law which typically seemed to burgeon by accident. Because of a clerical error he was made a barrister before he'd even completed half of his pupilage. Thrust backwards into the limelight he triumphed with his first case and was a huge success in his profession, unencumbered by training. This is typical of his life, which reads – in his autobiography at least – like an Italian version of *Tom Jones*.

Assailed by bandits, war, *amour fou*, penury and professional catastrophe he limped around Italy pursuing various adventures, throwing out the odd plot now and then for travelling theatre companies until in 1745 he received a commission to devise a play for a famous Harlequin. Thus *A Servant to Two Masters* was born as a scenario, pinned to the side of the stage, from which the *commedia dell'arte* troupe would improvise their play. The production was a huge success but when Goldoni finally came to see it he was appalled by the indulgence of the actors. In a fit of pique he wrote down a text for the players to learn and thus dealt the fatal blow to the centuries-old tradition of *commedia dell'arte*.

Commedia dell'arte, founded in Italy, was a popular theatrical tradition which became a transnational form during the Renaissance. Its improvised plays were performed by a company of actors; each one specialising in a stock character. The most famous of these characters was Harlequin. Harlequin was a *zanni*; a comic character, hailing from the mountains of Bergamo, who was both as thick as a post and sly as a fox and who specialised in all sorts of acrobatics. As the *commedia dell'arte* companies travelled round the different states in Italy they were forced to rely on visual forms of theatre to keep their audiences engaged no matter what language they actually spoke. In fact the companies themselves were sometimes made up of actors who spoke the specific dialects or languages from the various corners of Italy in which they were born. The plays were often (but not exclusively) performed in the open air and the heterogeneous crowd that gathered to watch saw a cross-section of their society which mirrored their own various origins.

Not only were the *commedia* plays a rattlebag of characters from different classes, they were also a jumble of styles. Actors who played the lovers would pride themselves on the beauty of their poesy, whilst the *zanni* would excel in the mechanics of slapstick motion. But the main theme of the plays was desire. Food, sex, love and money were the motors for the absurdly convoluted plots, and the players were never scared to explore the bodily baseness of these motivations. Harlequin frequently mimed eating himself because he was so hungry and is often depicted receiving an enema from a quack doctor. *Commedia*'s roots in the middle ages consistently showed through.

It was precisely this robustness that Goldoni desired to temper. In his opinion the *commedia dell'arte* had become decadent in the sense it was more concerned with the form of presentation than with the reality it represented. Goldoni's instinct was that of a realist, in the way that Ibsen and Chekhov were realists who sought to make the heightened drama of their day bear more resemblance to the reality of the bourgeois world they knew so well. And so for good or bad Goldoni stepped into the fray and attempted to deal with the realistic psychology of the *commedia dell'arte*'s stock of characters. He thus started a journey which led him to abandon the *commedia* conventions altogether, thus opening up a whole new world for the nineteenth century.

A Servant to Two Masters is pivotal to this revolution in the Italian theatre. But it seems crucially torn in its allegiances. The piece sounded the death-knell of *commedia dell'arte* at the same time as it revelled in its stagecraft and absurdities. It ushered in a new 'psychologism' of character whilst never letting the characters themselves escape the traditional trajectories of their comedic fates. In short, Goldoni was trying to serve both the *commedia* tradition and the current dragging him towards a realistic aesthetic more typical of the nineteenth century.

The play is full of *lazzi* – the moments such as Truffaldino serving the food and tearing up the letter – which were bravura flourishes that a skilled *zanni* would develop into a baroque set piece to delight audiences with his improvisatory skill and comic invention. Yet there is a tentative move towards making the crude excesses of the other characters more nuanced. The priapic indulgences of Pantaloon, which the *commedia dell'arte* revelled in, are softened to reveal a man internally torn rather than outwardly driven. (A distended phallus was an oft-used prop in some companies.) Indeed, some of the pathos which informed Goldoni's attempts as a tragedian seems to be embroidered throughout the piece.

Whilst the strengths of the play are so obviously grounded in its delight at theatrical mechanics, the plot rests on darker matter – a murder which has caused real loss and longing. Goldoni is juggling the dual enticements of a glorious confection on one hand and an attempt at emotional truth on the other. Any version of the play must recognise that it is neither a satisfactory *commedia dell'arte* piece nor a fully realised realistic world. It is impossible to realise its true value as a comedy without exploring its melancholy, and its melancholy is not sufficient meat without the sauce of *commedia*. Of the various versions that are played on the English stage none is entirely faithful to Goldoni. The most widely available is the French's version, prepared as a vehicle for Tommy Steele, which is quite simply a travesty. I was attracted to this master and servant play because I adapted Brecht's *Mr Puntila and his Man Matti* and was interested to investigate the genealogy of this relationship in an older play. However, instead of ripping the text apart to find the play anew as I'd done with the Brecht, I realised quite quickly that I would have to restore a work that has been worn down by our preconceptions, appropriations, additions and meddlings for many years. And so my project has been to reinstate the actual Goldoni play rather than create my own riff on it. I am the last to disparage anyone who wishes to stamp their own design on an old text, but since the director, Tim Supple, was drawn to the play not as a gagfest but as a drama, it seemed more appropriate to reinstate Goldoni than reiterate my own preoccupations.

I hope I haven't made too many claims for what is, and always was, an entertainment that delights in what developed later into farce. Disguises, muddled identifications, someone coming in the wrong door at the wrong time are all standbys for a simple good night out in the theatre – well, at least in my book. From Feydeau to Rix, farce has always been a form that poked fun at the hypocrisies of the middle classes. Goldoni certainly does that here, but there is a more unfamiliar drive to his writing. The comic resolution where all the couples are successfully paired is not for Goldoni simply a conservative endorsement of the status quo, or a cheap sentimental conclusion, but represents a profound longing for some kind of cohesive community. Goldoni was writing a year after the War of Austrian Succession and had been dragged into it himself and badly injured. This was more than a hundred years before the Risorgimento, and the turbulence of economic and political life made such happy endings in reality quite a rare event. I think we may read into what might seem a trite formula a wistful utopian sentiment where everyday exigencies of political division, hunger and economic instability are forgotten.

And so throughout every aspect of the piece Goldoni seems divided between these twin masters of a love of tradition and instinct for change. His life seems exemplary in trying to have one's cake and eat it; wanting to be both a lawyer and a dramatist, an instinctive conservative whilst being an accidental reformer. In the end Goldoni, who so celebrated the real people of Italy, was ironically driven out and ended his days in exile in Paris. He was condemned by the aristocratic playwright Carlo Gozzi as a radical for ruining traditional *commedia dell'arte*. And so he ended his days in Paris, as he says in his autobiography, with a 'stout stomach and a tender heart'. But the final act was far from uncomplicated. During the revolution he had his state pension discontinued because he was deemed to be an undoubted bourgeois influence. However, in true Goldoni form it was reinstated the very day before he died by the National Convention in recognition of his portrayals of the common man. And so maybe, like Truffaldino in the play, through luck as much as design Goldoni managed to serve conflicting ends simply through a mastery of common stagecraft. And in the process of killing off *commedia dell'arte* he has in fact served to keep it alive to this day.

Lee Hall
December 1999

A Servant to Two Masters

A Servant to Two Masters, a co-production between the Young Vic Theatre Company and the RSC, was first performed at The Other Place, Stratford-upon-Avon, on 8 December 1999, and at the Young Vic on 4 February 2000. The cast was as follows:

Clarice	Nikki Amuka-Bird
Florindo	Ariyon Bakare
Dr Lombardi/First Waiter	Geoffrey Beevers
Pantaloon/First Porter	Paul Bentall
Smeraldina/Waiter	Michelle Butterly
Beatrice	Claire Cox
Brighella/Second Porter	Kevork Malikyan
Silvio/Second Waiter	Orlando Seale
Truffaldino	Jason Watkins

Director Tim Supple
Designer Robert Innes Hopkins
Lighting Designer Paul Anderson
Sound Andrea J. Cox
Fights Malcolm Ranson
Dramaturg Simon Reade
Assistant Director Dan Milne
Traditional commedia consultant Andrea Cavarra (from Teatro del Vicolo)
Company voice work Andrew Wade
Production Managers Mark Graham/Paul Russell
Costume Supervisor Jenny Alden

Stage Manager Heidi Lennard
Deputy Stage Manager Maddy Grant
Assistant Stage Manager Paul Williams

Characters

Clarice; Florindo; Dr Lombardi; Pantaloon; Smeraldina; Beatrice; Brighella; Silvio; Truffaldino; First Waiter; Second Waiter; First Porter; Second Porter

Act One

Scene One

Pantaloon's *house*.

Pantaloon, **Dr Lombardi**, **Clarice**, **Silvio**, **Brighella**, **Smeraldina**.

Silvio   Here is my hand. And with it, I give you all my heart.

Pantaloon   Come along, my dove, let's have your hand now, we'll get you properly engaged and have you wed in no time.

Clarice   Dearest Silvio, I give you my hand and with it my promise to be your wife.

Silvio   And mine to be your husband.

Dr Lombardi   Excellent, that's all sorted then. No turning back now.

Smeraldina (*under her breath*)   The lucky cow. I wish it was me standing there.

Pantaloon   Smeraldina and Mr Brighella, I trust you will stand as witnesses to this betrothal here of Miss Clarice to Mr Silvio, the very distinguished son of our very good friend, Dr Lombardi.

Brighella   Indeed, it is an total honour and a privilege, sir.

Pantaloon   Well, it's only right and proper. After all I was the best man at your wedding, was I not. I know it's all a bit low-key. But the last thing you want is the relatives round on mass eating you out of house and home. No, we'll just have a nice quiet little meal together. Is that OK with you, my spooning sparrows?

Silvio   All I want is to be by your side.

Smeraldina   That's the tastiest dish for sure.

Dr Lombardi   We really don't go in for ceremony either. Do we, Silvio? No we Lombardis are ever vigilant against unnecessary pomp and circumstance et cetera. No, all that matters is that they love each other. And he thinks of nothing else, I can assure you.

Pantaloon   Well, I have to say this is a match made in heaven. If my prospective son-in-law, Federigo Rasponi, hadn't come to such a dreadful demise in Turin, Clarice would have been bound to marry him as I'd so meticulously arranged. As I say we had certain business arrangements together and he was, if I say so myself, quite a fine catch.

Silvio   Believe me, sir, I am fully aware of how fortunate I am. I can only hope that Clarice will say the same.

Clarice   Dearest Silvio, how could you bear to say that, you know I love you and even if I'd been forced to marry Rasponi my heart would always be yours.

Dr Lombardi   God moves in mysterious ways, eh? How did this Rasponi meet his unfortunate end?

Pantaloon   The poor sod was killed defending his sister's honour. Messy business, I understand. He was run through by the girl's lover and that, I'm afraid, was that.

Brighella   In Turin?

Pantaloon   In the very middle.

Brighella   I'm very sorry to hear it.

Pantaloon   Did you know this Federigo Rasponi?

Brighella   Oh, yes indeed. I was in Turin for three years and often saw his sister riding around on her horse. A very spirited young lady. Often dressed like a man to go riding. But Mr Federigo loved her, that's for sure. Who would have thought it?

Pantaloon   Oh well, the world's never short of a tragedy. Best not dwell too much on it. Tell you what, Mr Brighella, why don't you pop down to your kitchen and knock up a few choice specialities?

Brighella   Certainly, sir. An excellent idea. Though I say it myself, eat at Brighella's and you will have a feast fit for kings, today you will climb the summits of the culinary world and taste the finest delicacies known to man.

Pantaloon   Steady on there, just make sure there's something soft I can dip my bread in.

Knocking at the door.

Pantaloon   What's that?

Dr Lombardi   It's a knock on the door.

Pantaloon   Smeraldina. It's a knock on the door.

Smeraldina   I know.

Pantaloon   Could you see who it is, please?

Smeraldina   Keep your hair on.

She goes to the door.

Pantaloon   Let's hope it's not relatives, eh?

Clarice   Daddy, can we go now?

Pantaloon   Just hold your horses, darling, we'll just see who this is, and we'll all come with you.

Enter **Smeraldina**.

Smeraldina   It's a servant with a message, sir. He won't tell me anything and demands to see the master.

Pantaloon   Well, I am the master, send him up at once.

Smeraldina   All right. I'll show him up, sir.

Smeraldina *goes out again.*

Clarice   Please, Daddy, do we really have to stay?

Pantaloon   Where the devil are you thinking of going?

Clarice   I don't know. Anywhere. To my room.

Pantaloon   You must be joking, young lady. I'm not leaving those two lovebirds alone to peck each other into purgatory. Just stay here till we've sorted this out.

Dr Lombardi   Very wise, sir, take no chances.

Scene Two

Enter **Truffaldino** and **Smeraldina**.

Truffaldino   My most humblest salutations to you, ladies and gents. Ah, yes, a very fine company indeed, if you don't mind me saying so. The crème of the crème, if I'm not mistaken.

Pantaloon   And pray who are you, my good man?

Truffaldino   Please tell me who might be this fair young maiden?

Pantaloon   That's my daughter.

Truffaldino   May I offer my congratualtions, sir.

Smeraldina   And what's more she's just been engaged to be married.

Truffaldino   In that case I offer my commiserations. And who might you be, madam?

Smeraldina   I, sir, am my Lady's maid.

Truffaldino   In this case, I offer both my congratulations and commiserations.

Pantaloon   Come, sir, enough of this nonsense. What do you want? Who the devil are you? And who is your master?

Truffaldino A very good question, sir. Or may I say more correctly a very good set of questions. But given I am a simple man, may I advise you to take them one at a time.

Pantaloon The man's a total idiot.

Dr Lombardi Careful, Pantaloon, he might have some trick up his sleeve.

Truffaldino (*to* **Smeraldina**) I'm sorry, madam, but was it you or your master who was engaged?

Smeraldina Unfortunately it was my mistress.

Pantaloon Look. Either tell us who you are or be about your business.

Truffaldino If you simply wish to know who I am, I can settle the matter in two words, sir. My master's servant (three words, sir). (*Turning back to* **Smeraldina**.) As I was saying . . .

Pantaloon But who is your master?

Truffaldino A gentleman, sir. From another town who would like to pay his respects to you.

Pantaloon But who is this gentleman? What is his name?

Truffaldino Who, sir?

Pantaloon Your master.

Truffaldino For crying out loud. He is Federigo Rasponi of Turin, he sends his salutations, and he is awaiting downstairs to meet you. Satisified? (*To* **Smeraldina**.) Now where was we?

Pantaloon I beg your pardon, sir, but what the devil are you saying?

Truffaldino And if you are so interested I am Truffaldino Batocchio from the mountains of Bergamot.

Pantaloon I don't give a damn if you're from the Quantocks, sir.

Truffaldino   I beg your pardon?

Pantaloon   I want you to repeat your master's name.

Truffaldino   Poor old boy's deaf as worm. (*As if* **Pantaloon** *is deaf.*) My. Master. Is. Federigo. Rasp. Oni. Of. Turin. Sir.

Pantaloon   The man's out of his mind. Federigo Rasponi is dead.

Truffaldino   Dead?

Pantaloon   Dead. Defunct. Deceased. Demised. Kaput. No more, sir.

Truffaldino   Are you sure?

Pantaloon   I can tell you with complete certainty. He is absolutely, incontravertibly dead.

Dr Lombardi   I'm afraid, this is the case. No doubt about it.

Truffaldino   But this is terrible. Something awful must have happened. You'll have to excuse me. (*Aside.*) I better go and see if this is true.

Truffaldino *leaves.*

Pantaloon   What's going on here? Is this fellow playing the fool.

Dr Lombardi   I don't think he has the wit.

Brighella   Well, he is from Bergamot.

They all laugh superciliously.

Smeraldina   Well, I liked him. I thought he was quite attractive.

Pantaloon   It can't really be Federigo Rasponi?

Clarice   If it is, this is the most terrible news.

Pantaloon This isn't news, sweetheart. You saw the letters. The man's as dead as a door nail.

Silvio Even if he is alive and here in person. He's too late, anyway.

Enter **Truffaldino**.

Truffaldino This is an outrage. How I am served. Duped. Cruelly deluded. Is this the behaviour fitting of a gentleman, sir? I demand satisfaction.

Pantaloon Steady on now. What on earth's the matter?

Truffaldino You told me my master was dead.

Pantaloon And so he is.

Truffaldino 'And so he is'? He is downstairs, sir, as fit as a drayman's donkey. Still waiting to pay his respects, thank you very much.

Pantaloon Mr Federigo?

Truffaldino Mr Federigo.

Pantaloon Rasponi?

Truffaldino Rasponi.

Pantaloon Of Turin?

Truffaldino Of Bangalore. Of course, of Turin.

Pantaloon This is absolutely preposterous. Get out of here at once.

Truffaldino Hang on a minute, you pox-ridden little twit. (I said 'twit'.) Go and have a butcher's. He's down the stairs.

Pantaloon I'm not standing for this in my own house.

Truffaldino Please be seated, your honour.

Dr Lombardi Wait. Mr Pantaloon, sir. Let's not get embroiled in trivial recriminations. Let's have the fellow bring up this mysterious Rasponi, so we can see him with our own eyes.

Pantaloon   Yes, that'll fox you. Go on then, bring him back from the dead. You big baboon.

Truffaldino   Listen, perhaps he was dead. Perhaps he has been resurrected for all I know. But don't blame me. You can see for yourself. I've got no problem with that. But what I do have a problem with is your attitude, matey. You're lucky I'm from Bergamot where we have strict codes of honour. So this time I'll overlook it, smart-arse, but if I was you I'd watch your step.

Truffaldino *winks at* **Smeraldina** *as he leaves.*

Clarice   I'm shaking, Silvio.

Silvio   Don't worry, whatever happens you are mine.

Dr Lombardi   I say, it's quite a little mystery, isn't it.

Pantaloon   No doubt it's somebody trying on some sort of extortion.

Brighella   I knew the fella in Turin. I'll tell you if it's him or not.

Smeraldina   Well, I thought that little fella looked all right to me. I think I'll have a word with him. Excuse me, I just have to see a man about a dog in the courtyard, sir.

Smeraldina *leaves.*

Enter **Beatrice** *in man's clothing.*

Beatrice   Mr Pantaloon, it appears the courtesy which I have received in correspondence is not matched by your behaviour in person, having dutifully sent up my servant to gain an audience with you I am left standing this half-hour before you condescend to receive me.

Pantaloon   Sir, I beg your pardon. But may I enquire as to who you are?

Beatrice   Your humble servant, sir. Federigo Rasponi.

Pantaloon   Of Turin?

Beatrice   Of Turin.

General amazement.

Pantaloon   Well, we rejoice to see you alive and well, sir, after the dreadful news we received.

Beatrice   Indeed. It was given out that I was killed in a duel. But thanks be to heaven, I was merely wounded and quickly recovered, as you see. I immediately set out to Venice to meet our previous arrangements.

Pantaloon   I don't know quite what to say, sir, but unless you have concrete evidence to the contrary we have every reason to believe Federigo is dead.

Beatrice   You are quite right to be cautious in these ontological matters. And I am well aware that such arrangements need credentials. Here are four letters of introduction from various correspondents known to you. And one from the director of the bank. I think you will be satisfied.

Clarice   Oh, Silvio, we are lost.

Silvio   No. I will die before I lose you.

Brighella *is staring at* **Beatrice**.

Beatrice   Do I know you, sir?

Brighella   Indeed, sir. Surely you recognise Brighella Cavicchio. From Turin, sir?

Beatrice (*aside*)   Please don't give me away. Oh, yes, of course. What brings you here?

Brighella   I keep an inn, sir. At your service.

Beatrice   Brighella Cavicchio. What excellent luck, I will lodge with you for certain.

Brighella   It'd be a pleasure, sir.

Pantaloon   Well, they certainly appear to be in order. And as you've presented them in person, I have no other option but to accept you.

Beatrice   If you have any lingering doubts I'm sure Mr Brighella can vouch that I am, indeed, a Rasponi.

Brighella   That I can.

Pantaloon   That settles it. I must ask for a pardon, sir, I have done you a great disservice.

Clarice   So this really is Federigo Rasponi?

Pantaloon   The very man.

Clarice   Oh this is terrible.

Silvio   Listen, you are mine and I will let no man tear us asunder.

Pantaloon   Well, that's what I call timing.

Dr Lombardi   *Accidit in puncto, quod non contigit in anno.* Or so they say.

Beatrice   But tell me, sir. Who is this lady?

Pantaloon   This is Clarice, my daughter.

Beatrice   The daughter promised to me in marriage?

Pantaloon   The same, sir.

Beatrice   Ma'am, permit me to say I am honoured.

Clarice   Your most humble servant.

Beatrice   A rather cool reception.

Pantaloon   I'm afraid it's rather par for the course. She's timid by nature.

Beatrice   And this gentleman is also your relation?

Pantaloon   Well, yes. I suppose he is my nephew.

Silvio   No, sir. I am nobody's nephew. I am the husband of his daughter. Miss Clarice.

Dr Lombardi   That's my boy. Say your piece, son, but careful he looks like a bit of a bruiser.

Beatrice   I beg your pardon, sir, but how can you be Clarice's husband when she was promised to me?

Pantaloon   All right, all right. I'll come clean. Dear Mr Rasponi, sir, convinced of your very sad and tragic demise I have given my daughter to Mr Silvio here with the best intentions in the world. But thanks be to God, you arrive in the nick of time, and of course, I am now bound to keep my word. Mr Silvio, I don't know what to say. Surely you can appreciate an old man's predicament and know I mean you no ill will whatsoever.

Silvio   But surely Federigo Rasponi will never consent to marry a lady who has already given her hand?

Beatrice   As long as her dowry's intact, I couldn't care less, sir.

Dr Lombardi   A very fashionable attitude, I must say.

Beatrice   I trust Miss Clarice will not refuse my hand?

Silvio   But you are too late. Clarice is mine and I will never give her up. And should you do me wrong, Mr Pantaloon, I will take my revenge upon you, and anyone who tries to take Clarice from me will reckon with this sword.

Silvio *exits*.

Dr Lombardi   Bravo, by God.

Beatrice   Isn't it a little drastic?

Dr Lombardi   With all due respect, sir, I think you have arrived too late. And I'm afraid Clarice will have to marry my son. The law is quite clear on this point. *Prior in tempore, potior in iure.*

Exit **Dr Lombardi**.

Beatrice   And you, good Lady Bride, haven't you anything to say?

Clarice   Only that you have ruined my entire life.

Exit **Clarice**.

Pantaloon   Oh the insolent little minx!

Pantaloon *goes to pursue her, but is stopped by* **Beatrice**.

Beatrice   Please, sir. This is not the time to reproach her. I have no doubt that in good time I will win her affections but in the meantime I think we should go over the accounts of our business arrangements; which must, you will agree, be sorted out whatever happens.

Pantaloon   Everything is in order, I can assure you, and we can settle up the money I owe you whenever it suits you, sir.

Beatrice   Excellent. I'll call again once I'm settled in. But if you'll excuse me, Mr Brighella and I have a little business we must attend to.

Pantaloon   As you wish, sir, but if you are in need of anything, anything at all, I am at your disposal.

Beatrice   Well, if it's not too much trouble perhaps you could furnish me with a little cash to tide me over, I'd be enormously obliged.

Pantaloon   At once, at once, sir. I'd be delighted. My cashier, Michael Cassio, will be here forthwith and soon as he arrives I'll have some money sent over to Brighella's.

Beatrice   Thank you. But really, I'll have my servant drop by. Don't worry, he's an honourable chap. You can trust him with anything.

Pantaloon   If you say so, sir.

Beatrice   Well, I must be about my business. Until later.

Pantaloon   Your most humble servant, sir.

Scene Three

Beatrice *and* **Brighella** *are alone.*

Brighella   Miss Beatrice, I presume.

Beatrice   For heaven's sake, please, don't undo me now, Brighella. My poor brother has been killed by my lover, Florindo Aretusi. Florindo has fled from justice and now I'm left to wander in misery in the hope of finding him. But knowing Federigo was bound for Venice to marry the young girl, I have borrowed my brother's clothing and some letters of identification, and with the money I will get from Pantaloon I'll be able to track Florindo down. Please, Brighella, please don't give me away. I will reward you generously for your pains.

Brighella   It's all very well but I don't want to be seen as responsible for Mr Pantaloon being swindled out of a fortune.

Beatrice   What do you mean 'swindled'? For God's sake that money is rightfully mine. Am I not my brother's heir?

Brighella   Well, in that case, just tell him who you are.

Beatrice   And end up with nothing? You've seen him. The first thing he'd do is start clucking like a mother hen and have me sent home. No, I will have my freedom as brief as it may be. Please, Brighella, take me as a man.

Brighella   Well, I always said you had a lot of spunk. Trust me. Brighella is at your service. 'Sir.'

Beatrice   Shall we go to your inn?

Brighella   What about your servant?

Beatrice   He's in the street.

Brighella   Where on earth did you happen to meet such an 'interesting' fellow?

Beatrice   I picked him up on the way here. I know he looks a bit stupid, but actually, I think he's rather loyal.

Brighella   Well, at least he's got one good quality. We better go. The things we do for love, Mr Beatrice?

Beatrice   Believe me. Love could drive me to far greater excesses.

Brighella   Please. Don't let me stop you. It's better than a night in the theatre.

They leave.

Scene Four

The street in front of **Brighella**'s *inn.* **Truffaldino**. *His belly rumbles.*

Truffaldino   It's just not on, is it? I'm sick of this for a lark. I've had some stingy swines in my time but this takes the biscuit. I'll be lucky to see a bowl of gruel from one week's end to the next with this fella. It's not even twelve o' clock and I'm on starvation point. I mean the first thing you do when you get into town is put your feet up and get some decent scran down your neck, don't you? But oh no, not Lord Anorexia here. No, he's pissed off down the quay to get his trunk, et cetera, et cetera; I could have passed on for all he cares. If I only had some dosh I'd sod the skinny sod; nip in there and give me gnashers a bit of training out of me own back pocket. But have I seen any wages? Have I buggery. I'm stood round here like one o'clock half struck, and bloody well famished. I could have been somebody, you know. I could have been a contender.

Enter **Florindo** *followed by a* **Porter** *carrying a trunk on his back.*

Porter   I can't go any further. It's killing me.

Florindo   Look, just another few steps, you're nearly there.

Porter   I can't, I can't. It's slipping.

Florindo   I told you you weren't up to it.

Truffaldino   Can I help there, sir?

Florindo   For God's sake grab that end and take it into the inn.

Truffaldino   Right you are, sir.

Truffaldino *grabs the trunk, it's heavier than he thought, but pushes the* **Porter** *out of the way.*

Truffaldino (*to the* **Porter**)   Now bugger off, will you.

Florindo   Bravo, that man.

Truffaldino   There you go, sir, a piece of cake.

Truffaldino *exits into the inn.*

Florindo (*to the* **Porter**)   See. That wasn't very difficult at all.

Porter   But I'm an old man, sir. I wasn't meant to be a porter. I was reduced to it. I was quite respectable in my day, sir.

Florindo   You are a waste of space, man.

Florindo *turns to go in.* **Truffaldino** *comes out.*

Truffaldino   All done and dusted, sir.

Porter   Excuse me.

Florindo *looks at him in amazement.*

Florindo   What now?

Porter   Something for my labour, sir.

Florindo   What labour? I'll give you something 'for your labour, sir'. A good kick up the arse. Now get out of it before you're arrested.

Florindo *gives the* **Porter** *a kick and he goes off terrified.*

Truffaldino   Like I say, sir, you just can't get the staff these days, can you?

Florindo   Have you any idea what this place is like?

Truffaldino   Oh, a top-notch establishment this, sir. Nice comfy beds, an excellent cellar, and, mmm, a delicious smell of food coming from the kitchen. Just mention my name and you and your servant, sir, will be served like aristocracy.

Florindo   And your name is . . . ?

Truffaldino   Truffaldino Battachio.

Florindo   And what line of work are you in?

Truffaldino   Well . . . erm . . . service, sir.

Florindo   Are you indeed. And at this moment, are you gainfully employed?

Truffaldino *looks around.*

Truffaldino   Well, no, not at this moment. (It's not exactly a lie, is it.)

Florindo   So you're without a master?

Truffaldino   Here I stand, sir. I can do no other.

Florindo   Well, do you want to be my servant?

Truffaldino   It's very hard to say, sir. What terms are we talking about?

Florindo   Terms? What do people usually pay?

Truffaldino   Well, my other master, I mean, the one who I am no longer employed by, paid a ducat a day.

Florindo   A ducat a day.

Truffaldino   But, of course, a man of my calibre, and undeniable charm, sir, is always looking to better himself.

Florindo   A ducat a day and a ha'penny's worth of baccy.

Truffaldino   And a nice little ham sandwich of a lunchtime.

Florindo   Done. All your meals will be taken care of.

Truffaldino   It's a pleasure doing business with you.

Florindo   I suppose you can furnish me with the requisite references.

Truffaldino   I beg your pardon, sir?

Florindo   You don't expect me to take you on without someone to vouch for you?

Truffaldino   No problem at all. Just nip up to Bergamot, there's plenty of people know me there, sir.

Florindo   But we're in Venice.

Truffaldino   Ah, I never thought of that. Look, we could forget about the tobacco.

Florindo   OK, I'll give you a go, but listen, any monkey business and you're for the high jump. Understood?

Truffaldino   Indupidipipably, your honour, sir.

Florindo   Just go down to the post office and collect any letters that may have been sent for Florindo Aretusi. And bring them here, toot sweet, understood.

Truffaldino   What about the ham sandwich, sir?

Florindo   When you are gone. I'll order lunch.

Truffaldino   Very good indeed, sir.

As **Florindo** *leaves.*

Florindo (*aside*)   Cheeky little sod, aren't you. We'll see how it goes.

Scene Five

Truffaldino, *then* **Beatrice** *and* **Brighella**.

Truffaldino   Just call me Mr Machiavelli. A ducat a day.
I'd be lucky to escape malnutrition with the other bugger.
Well, seeing Mr Bumfluff is not at hand, I may as well nip
down the old post office and earn a decent living for a
change.

Beatrice   Where are you going? Is this what you call
waiting here patiently for me.

Truffaldino   Terribly sorry, sir. I was just, er, stretching
my legs.

Beatrice   How do you expect me to find you. If you go
walkabout every five minutes.

Truffaldino   I was just trying desperately to stave off my
hunger, sir.

Beatrice   Listen, if you want any lunch at all, you will get
down to the landing stage and bring up my trunk to
Brighella's immediately.

Truffaldino (*of the inn*)   That one there?

Beatrice   That one there. And if I were you, I'd be smart
about it. And while you're at it go to the post office and
enquire if there are any letters for me. Infact enquire if there
are any letters also, for my sister. She was supposed to be
coming with me, then something came up. Anyway, you
never know who might be writing to her expecting an
immediate reply. So away you go, there's a good man. Just
see if there's anything for a Miss Beatrice while you're there.

Brighella (*to* **Beatrice**)   But who will be writing to you
here?

Beatrice   I asked my faithful steward to send me any
news that could help me. (*To* **Truffaldino**.) Look, get a
move on or the place [*city*] will have sunk.

Truffaldino   And who are you?

Brighella   I'm the innkeeper, now off you go and I'll sort you out with a nice bit of lunch when you get back.

Beatrice *and* **Brighella** *go off.*

Truffaldino   Bloody brilliant. There are vast ranks of the unemployed looking in vain for a master and I go and land myself with two of the buggers. What am I going do now? I can't look after both, can I? I suppose I'd get double the pay, and two suppers, and to be quite honest, it's something to be proud of, isn't it. Streamlined efficiency, a sort of downsizing of the service economy. If they'd have thought it up, it'd be called innovation. That settles it. I'm off to the post office. Twice.

Enter **Silvio**.

Silvio   Ah, my good man. Could I have a word with you.

Truffaldino   Bloody hell. Not another one.

Silvio   Where is your master?

Truffaldino   My master?

Silvio   You do have a master, do you not?

Truffaldino   Er, yes, sir. He's in the inn.

Silvio   Well, go tell him, that I want to have a word.

Truffaldino   But, sir –

Silvio (*shouts*)   Tell him I want a word or else.

Truffaldino   But –

Silvio   One more sound and I'll cut that tongue out of your slavering mouth.

Truffaldino   But which master do you want?

Silvio   That's it.

Silvio *lunges at* **Truffaldino** *who escapes.*

Truffaldino (*aside*)   I'll just have to take pot luck.

Truffaldino *goes*.

Silvio   I am not going to stand for any rivals. Federigo may have got off once with his life, but I promise it won't happen again. Either he drops all pretensions to Clarice or I will cut his heart out. Who on earth is this?

Silvio *withdraws as* **Truffaldino** *enters with* **Florindo**.

Truffaldino   There he is, sir. Watch it. He's a nutcase.

Florindo   Who's this? I've never seen the fellow in my life.

Truffaldino   I don't know nothing, sir. And by your leave I will go for those letters, sir. I'm not getting mixed up in this.

Truffaldino *exits*.

Silvio   Where the hell is this Federigo?

Florindo (*to himself*)   Well, here goes. (*To* **Silvio**.) Are you the man who has been calling for me?

Silvio   I'm afraid not, sir. I have not had the honour of your aquaintance.

Florindo   Yet my servant who just left informed me you were issuing threats and provoking me to a challenge.

Silvio   He misunderstood, sir. I wished to speak to his master.

Florindo   Well, I am his master.

Silvio   You, sir?

Florindo   Indeed.

Silvio   Then, I must beg for your pardon, sir, either your man is the double of one I saw this morning, or this man waits on someone else.

Florindo   I can assure you, sir. The man waits on me.

Silvio   In that case please accept my humble apologies and we'll make no more of the matter.

Florindo   No harm done. These things happen.

Silvio   Are you a stranger here, sir?

Florindo   From Turin, actually, at your service.

Silvio   How amazing. The man I would speak to is also from Turin.

Florindo   Maybe I could help you. I may know the man and would only be too happy to see you have satisfaction, sir.

Silvio   Do you know, then, a certain Federigo Rasponi.

Florindo   Only too well.

Silvio   He insolently makes, on some previous pretext with her father, claim to my fiancée who only this morning publicly gave me her hand.

Florindo   Please, let me allay your fears. Federigo cannot take your wife from you, because he is dead.

Silvio   So everyone thought, sir, but this morning he turned up here in Venice, very much alive.

Florindo   Alive! I am dumbstruck.

Silvio   You're not the only one.

Florindo   But I can assure you, sir, he is dead.

Silvio   But I can assure you, sir, he is alive.

Florindo   But you must be mistaken.

Silvio   Master Pantaloon Parsimoni, father of my betrothed, made all possible enquiries to ascertain the man's identity, and he had incontestable proofs, sir.

Florindo (*aside*)   So he wasn't killed after all.

Silvio   And so, he either abandons his claims to Clarice or I will end his life for sure.

Florindo   I came all the way to Venice only to be haunted by him here.

Silvio   I am surprised you haven't met him. He is supposedly lodging in that inn.

Florindo   I haven't seen a soul. I was told there were no other guests here.

Silvio   Maybe he has changed his mind. I'm sorry to have troubled you. But I trust if you come across the scoundrel you will, for his own welfare, persuade him to abandon all claims to my wife. I am Silvio Lombardi, and for ever, your humble servant, sir. And might I discover your name?

Florindo   Oh, er, Fusilli Arrabiata, your obediant servant.

Silvio   Master Arrabiata, I am yours to command.

Silvio *exits*.

Scene Six

Florindo   How is this possible? I felt the sword pierce to the bone with my own hand. With my own eyes I saw him drowned in his blood. How could he have survived? Perhaps I fled too quickly and he was resurrected without my knowledge. And now I have left my beloved Beatrice to die with sorrow at my disappearance. Oh I must go straight back and console her grieving soul.

Scene Seven

Enter **Truffaldino** *and a* **Porter** *carrying* **Beatrice***'s trunk. They see* **Florindo** *and they jump out of sight.*

Truffaldino   Get down – Christ. There's the other master. Back a bit. Wait here. (*To* **Florindo**.) Wotcha, guv.

Florindo   Truffaldino, we must leave for Turin.

Truffaldino   I beg you pardon, sir?

Florindo   At once, now. We're leaving for Turin.

Truffaldino   But we haven't had dinner.

Florindo   Well, we must eat quickly and be on our way.

Truffaldino   This might cost you a bit extra, you realise.

Florindo   Never mind the expense, this is important. Did you go to the post office?

Truffaldino   Indeed I did, sir.

Florindo   Well?

Truffaldino   I have something for you right here, sir.

Florindo   Where is it?

Truffaldino   I'm just looking.

He pulls out three letters.

Oh flummery. They're all mixed up. I knew I should've learned to read.

Florindo   What are you doing, man. Give me my letters.

Truffaldino   Right away, sir. (*Aside.*) Bollocks. (*To* **Florindo**.) I have to warn you, sir, but not all of the letters are for you.

Florindo   What do you mean?

Truffaldino   On approaching the post, sir, I happened upon another servant who I knew from Bergamot, sir, and he asked me to retrieve some letters for his master, you know, to save him the trouble, sir, as he is a very busy man, the other servant. And, er, his letters are here too.

Florindo   Give them here.

Truffaldino   Terribly sorry.

Florindo (*aside*)   What is this? To Beatrice Rasponi. (*To* **Truffaldino**.) What is this?

Truffaldino   That must be the one for my mate.

Florindo   Who is this 'mate' exactly?

Truffaldino   A servant, sir, name of . . . Pasqual.

Florindo   Pasqual!

Truffaldino   Yes, sir, a very fine friend, sir.

Florindo   Whom does he serve?

Truffaldino   Don't know, sir.

Florindo   But how could you have retrieved the letters without his master's name?

Truffaldino   Very good point, sir. (*Aside.*) Shit!

Florindo   What was the name?

Truffaldino   It's slipped my mind, sir.

Florindo   What mind?

Truffaldino   I had it on a bit of paper, sir.

Florindo   Well, where is the bit of paper?

Truffaldino   At the post office. (*Aside.*) You won't catch me out.

Florindo   Well, where is this Pasqual?

Truffaldino (*aside*)   Bollox. (*To* **Florindo**.) I haven't the foggiest.

Florindo   How on earth did you expect to deliver this letter to him?

Truffaldino   We arranged to meet at the piazza.

Florindo   This is ridiculous.

Truffaldino   And if you'll give me the letter I'll take it there forthwith. (*Aside.*) A beautiful move.

Florindo   No. I think I will open the letter.

Truffaldino   No. Oh, please, please don't open the letter, sir. It is a grevious offence, sir, to open people's letters.

Florindo   I don't care who I offend. This letter is addressed to someone who is dearer to me than my own soul. I have no scruples here.

Truffaldino   Oh Christ.

Florindo (*reading*)   'My Illustrious Milady, news of your departure has set the whole town of a fire and the general consensus is that you have gone abroad after Mr Florindo. The court what have discovered that you are abroad in a man's dress are doing their utmost to have you arrested. I did not send the letter immediately from the suspected place of correspondence but did give this missive to a friend who posted it to you on account of avoiding any such tracings or other such which might inevitably befall you. Any further news and I shall write to you by the same. Your humble, obediant and truly faithful servant, ever yours with everlasting honour, Antonio della Dorio. PS This letter was penned by the chambermaid, Mistress Pantone, on my humble behalf.

Truffaldino   Very well writ if you don't mind me saying so.

Florindo   This is unbelievable. Beatrice abroad. Dressed as a man. To join me. Oh my sweet angel, if only there is a way to find her here in Venice.

(*To* **Truffaldino**.) Truffaldino, you must find this Pasqual and the person he serves, find out where they are lodged, bring him here to me and I will give you more money than you've ever dreamed of.

Truffaldino   Well, thank you very much, sir. And maybe a bit of lunch, eh?

Florindo *gives* **Truffaldino** *the letter.*

Florindo   Here. I am relying on you completely. This matter is of infinite importance to me.

Truffaldino   I can't give it back like this.

Florindo   Tell him there was an accident or something, don't make difficulties, make haste.

Truffaldino   So we're not going to Turin I take it?

Florindo   Stop wasting precious time. (*Aside.*) Beatrice in Venice. Federigo in Venice. If her brother catches me there'll be hell to pay. I'll have to do everything to track her down myself.

Florindo *leaves.*

Scene Eight

Truffaldino (*very pleased with himself*)   I just can't help myself. Seeing how well I'm doing I may as well give this double service thing a proper run round the block. A man of my singular potential, it seems, is up to anything. But I can't get away with giving this thing back in this state. Let's see if I can fold it so they won't notice.

He makes a pig's ear of it.

That's better, but it needs sticking. How the hell do I wangle that? Maybe I could chew up a bit of bread as a sort of mortar, and then stick it like me granny used to do with her false teeth.

He fishes in his pocket and pulls out a bit of bread.

I'll give it a go. Well, there goes the emergency rations, but que sera sera as they say in England.

He chews the bread but inadvertently swallows it.

Oh bugger. There's hardly any left now.

Chews it and swallows some more.

It's just not natural to have to do this. One last go.

He manages not to swallow it and unwillingly removes it from his mouth.

Got you. Now to seal the bastard.

He seals the flap with bread.

Champion. Look at that. Top-notch. Oh Christ. The bloody porter.

He goes to the wing.

Hey, come on with that trunk.

Porter   I thought you'd never ask. Where d'ya want it, guv.

Truffaldino   Quick, get it over there, I'll be in in a mo.

Porter   Hang on a minute, who's going to pay for all this humping?

Scene Nine

Enter **Beatrice** *from the inn.*

Beatrice   Is that my trunk?

Truffaldino   Yes. I think so.

Beatrice   Take it up to my room.

Porter   But which is your room, sir?

Beatrice   I don't know. Ask the waiter.

Porter   Here, wait a minute. There's three and six to pay on this.

Beatrice   Look, just get it upstairs pronto or you'll be getting a kick up the backside.

Porter   Listen, I've been stood round for half a bleeding hour. I want me money before I move another inch.

Beatrice   Look, my good man. This really isn't a good time.

Porter   I've got a good mind to drop this in the middle of the street.

Beatrice *gives him a look of authoritative disdain and the* **Porter** *is chastened. He scuttles off without another word.*

Truffaldino   Charming fellows these Venetians.

Beatrice   Have you been to the post office?

Truffaldino   Indeed I have, sir.

Beatrice   Any letters for me?

Truffaldino   None at all. But there was one for your sister, sir.

Beatrice   Give it here at once.

Truffaldino   Here you go.

Beatrice   This letter's been opened.

Truffaldino   Opened. No, it isn't possible.

Beatrice   Opened and sealed with bread.

Truffaldino   How on earth could that have happened?

Beatrice   You insolent blaggard. Who opened this letter?

Truffaldino   Please, sir. I'll confess. We all make mistakes and there was a letter for me at the post and since I can't read I opened your letter by mistake. It was a dreadful thing and I should be flogged, sir, beaten and flogged and quartered, but please know it was a humble mistake, sir.

Beatrice   Well, I suppose there's been no harm done.

Truffaldino   I'm a very simple man, sir.

Beatrice   Did you read this letter? Do you know what it says?

Truffaldino   Not a word.

Beatrice   Has anyone else seen it?

Truffaldino (*indignant*)   Oh!

Beatrice   Has anyone seen it?

Truffaldino   Perish the very thought, sir.

Beatrice   If you're lying . . . (*She reads the letter.*)

Truffaldino (*aside*)   Well, that didn't go *too* badly.

Beatrice   Antonio, you are no scholar but you are a good man.

(*To* **Truffaldino**.)   Now, Truffaldino, there is a certain matter I must attend to and I want you to go into the inn, open the trunk – here are the keys – unpack my clothes and give them an airing. And then when I get back we'll have lunch.

Truffaldino   Hallelujah.

Beatrice (*to herself*)   I better check up on Pantaloon and that money he owes me.

Beatrice *goes out.*

Scene Ten

Truffaldino   I don't know how I get away with it. I'll have to start putting my fees up.

Enter **Pantaloon**.

Pantaloon   Ah, my good man, is your master at home?

Truffaldino   No, sir. I'm afraid he ain't.

Pantaloon   Have you any idea where he's gone?

Truffaldino   Not the foggiest, sir.

Pantaloon   Well, will he be back for lunch?

Truffaldino   I should bloody well hope so.

Pantaloon   In that case, as soon as he returns make sure he gets this. There's a hundred ducats there. It should tide him over for a couple of days. I'm afraid I can't stop. Make sure he gets it. Good day.

Exit **Pantaloon**.

Scene Eleven

Truffaldino   Hang on a minute. Wait. Bon voyage, then. He never said which master.

Enter **Florindo**.

Florindo   Well, have you found Pasqual?

Truffaldino   No, not exactly, but I met a man who gave me a hundred ducats.

Florindo   A hundred ducats. What the devil for?

Truffaldino   I haven't the foggiest. You weren't expecting a hundred ducats, were you?

Florindo   I don't know. I suppose I did present a letter of credit to a merchant this morning.

Truffaldino   So the money's yours?

Florindo   Well, what did this fellow say?

Truffaldino   He said give it to your master.

Florindo   Well, of course it's my money, you incompetent dolt.

Truffaldino   I was just checking.

Florindo Now for the love of God stop messing about and go and find Pasqual.

Truffaldino No, I can't, sir.

Florindo I beg your pardon.

Truffaldino Not on an empty stomach. Please, sir, just a tiny little morsel and I'll be off like a bloodhound.

Florindo All right, all right. I'll order right away.

Florindo *goes in.*

Truffaldino Bloody hell. At least I've done one thing right today.

Scene Twelve

A room in **Pantaloon**'*s house.*

Pantaloon It's no use. You're marrying Federigo Rasponi whether you like it or not. I have given him my word and there's the long and the short of it.

Clarice Please, Daddy. This is absolute tyranny.

Pantaloon I'll not have you using that sort of language. You were quite happy with the arrangement when it was first proposed, you can't go chopping and changing now whenever it suits you.

Clarice But the only reason I consented was out of obedience to you.

Pantaloon So why refuse me now?

Clarice I simply can't do it.

Pantaloon What do you mean: 'can't do it'?

Clarice Nothing will make me take Federigo.

Pantaloon Nothing? What's the matter with him?

Clarice   I hate him.

Pantaloon   Come on, sweetness. I mean, he has his good points.

Clarice   Daddy, I am sworn to Silvio.

Pantaloon   Please, my little duckling, put Silvio out of your mind and consider Federigo on his own merits.

Clarice   I can't put Silvio out of my mind. All I see, all I think, all I feel is Silvio. My entire world is Silvio and you were the first to approve him.

Pantaloon   Oh my poor lamb. Don't you see? You have to make a virtue out of necessity.

Clarice   How can I 'make' anything? Now I am nothing?

Pantaloon   Please, please, my poor child.

Enter **Smeraldina**.

Smeraldina   Sir, Master Federigo is here and desperate to see you.

Pantaloon   Send him up, I am at his service.

Clarice   Oh this is unbearable.

Smeraldina   You silly thing. What on earth are you upset about? Ma'am. I'd give my right arm to be in your position.

Pantaloon   Come on, my sweet thing, don't let him see you cry.

Clarice   What am I supposed to do? My heart is burst open.

Scene Thirteen

Beatrice   My greatest respects, Mr Pantaloon.

Pantaloon   Ever your humble servant, sir, I trust you received the hundred ducats.

Beatrice   I'm afraid I did not.

Pantaloon   I gave it to your man only just now. You did say he was to be trusted.

Beatrice   No cause for alarm. I just haven't caught up with him yet. Is anything wrong?

Pantaloon   Please, Mr Rasponi, you must understand that the news of your death has affected her greatly. We are sure she'll get over it in time.

Beatrice   Perhaps if I spoke to her alone, I might be able to bring her round.

Pantaloon   Yes, of course, I'll leave you for a moment. Clarice, I'll be back shortly, I want you to try and be nice to your future husband for me. Come on, try to be sensible.

Exit **Pantaloon**.

Scene Fourteen

Beatrice   My dear lady . . .

Clarice   Get away. I don't want you anywhere near me.

Beatrice   Those are cruel words to give your future husband.

Clarice   Even if they drag me screaming and kicking to the altar I will never love you.

Beatrice   Please, just listen and you won't hate me for long.

Clarice   I shall hate you, sir, to the end of eternity.

Beatrice   You don't even know who I am.

Clarice   I know you, sir, you are the destroyer of my life.

Beatrice   But, really, I can console you.

Clarice   Don't flatter yourself. Silvio is my sole consolation.

Beatrice   Look, I'm not saying I can do what Silvio does, but I can make you happy.

Clarice   Are you such a monster you'll ignore everything I say?

Beatrice   Please.

Clarice   I'll scream the place down.

Beatrice   Just let me share a secret.

Clarice   I will share nothing with you.

Beatrice   Oh for God's sake just let me get a word in edgeways.

Clarice   You monstrous egotistical bastard! You've ruined everything.

Beatrice   Listen, you have no desire for me. I have no desire for you. You have given your hand to another, I have to another given my heart.

Clarice   Maybe you're not so bad after all.

Beatrice   That's what I've been trying to tell you since I came in.

Clarice   Is this some kind of joke?

Beatrice   I've never been so serious in my whole life. And if you swear to keep this a secret I can completely put your mind at rest.

Clarice   OK. I swear.

Beatrice   I am not Federigo. I am his sister, Beatrice.

Clarice   What? A woman?

Beatrice   A woman.

Clarice   But what about your brother?

Beatrice   Killed in the fight. The man I love was blamed for his death and it's him I am desperate to find here. I thought I'd stand more chance as a man. But please, by all the sacred laws of love and charity, do not betray me. I know it was a bit rash to tell you, but you seemed to be getting hysterical. And to make matters worse, your sweet Silvio has threatened to slit me navel to chops, which you will admit is not entirely in my best interests.

Clarice   I'll tell him at once.

Beatrice   No you will not.

Clarice   Won't I?

Beatrice   I'm absolutely counting on you. You mustn't tell a soul. And to be quite honest, it would make life a lot easier if you were just a little more civil towards me.

Clarice   Civil. I will be your greatest friend. I'll do anything you ask.

Beatrice   Look, I pledge my eternal friendship. Give me your hand.

Clarice   I beg your pardon

Beatrice   Are you afraid I'm lying? I'll give you incontrovertible proof.

Clarice   This is a dream.

Beatrice   Well, it isn't exactly the kind of thing that happens every day, is it.

Clarice   Extraordinary. Extraordinary.

Beatrice   Look, I must go. Let's embrace in honest friendship.

Clarice I doubt you no longer.

Enter **Pantaloon**.

Scene Fifteen

Pantaloon Oh, praise the lord. Nice work, there, if you don't mind me saying so. I see you've sharp changed your tune.

Beatrice Did I not say I'd win her round?

Pantaloon Well, I take my hat off to you. You've done in four minutes what would've taken me four years. We'll see to the wedding right away then.

Clarice (*aside*) Oh, this is worse than ever. (*To* **Pantaloon**.) Please, there's no need to hurry, Daddy.

Pantaloon What? Messing around in here like a couple of polecats. Listen, I'm taking no chances, you're getting hitched tomorrow and that's final.

Beatrice Of course, it's completely necessary to get all the financial arrangements out of the way first.

Pantaloon Don't worry, we'll have it sorted out in no time.

Clarice But Daddy . . .

Pantaloon I'll pop over and tell Silvio right away.

Clarice Please, no. He'll go crazy.

Pantaloon What, are you after both of them?

Clarice But Daddy . . .

Pantaloon No more buts. It's decided. I am ever your humble servant, sir.

He starts to leave.

You're man and wife now and that's the end of it.

Clarice   But . . .

Pantaloon   We'll talk about it later.

He exits.

Scene Sixteen

Clarice   Brilliant.

Beatrice   Don't worry. We'll work something out.

Clarice   This is more of a mess than before.

Beatrice   I'll think of something.

Clarice   And what do you want me to do until then? What about poor Silvio? What do you expect us to do?

Beatrice   Oh, for God's sake, just suffer for a while.

Clarice   I don't think I can bear this.

Beatrice   Well, bear it you must. I can assure you your present woes will make your future joy the sweeter.

Beatrice *leaves.*

Clarice   How can I think of future happiness when I am lost in such present pain. Why is life so much endless hoping and insufferable desire and so little actual joy.

Act Two

Scene One

A courtyard, **Pantaloon**'s *house.*

Silvio Leave me alone.

Dr Lombardi Wait. Silvio.

Silvio I'm warning you.

Dr Lombardi What do you think you're doing prowling round Pantaloon's courtyard?

Silvio Either he'll keep his word or I'll force him to reap the consequences.

Dr Lombardi Silvio, this is the man's own house. You're making a complete fool of yourself.

Silvio No. He's making a fool of me. He deserves no civility from us.

Dr Lombardi That might be true – but it's no reason to be running around like some rabid dog. Please, let me have a word with him and perhaps a little reason will remind him where his duties lie. Why don't you just slip off somewhere, out of this courtyard, I'll talk to Pantaloon and be with you forthwith.

Silvio But . . .

Dr Lombardi No buts. Just do as I say.

Silvio This once. I'll be waiting at the coffee bar but if he persists, I swear I'll skewer that fat gut of his.

Silvio *exits.*

Dr Lombardi Oh my poor boy. How could they do this if there was any doubt about the Turinese gentleman's eschatological status. But what is required here is to deal with this in a completely rational and objective manner.

Enter **Pantaloon**.

Pantaloon   What the devil are you doing here?

Dr Lombardi   Ah, Mr Pantaloon, my greatest respects.

Pantaloon   I was just on my way to see you.

Dr Lombardi   Excellent. I expect you were hurrying with the news that Clarice will indeed marry dear Silvio.

Pantaloon   Well, actually . . .

Dr Lombardi   No need for explantions, I totally appreciate the delicacy of the difficult imbroglio you were placed in. But as we're old friends let's put the matter completely behind us.

Pantaloon   Well, the fact is . . .

Dr Lombardi   I would be the first to admit that you were taken totally by surprise and had no time to consider the obvious and grievous wrong you were to perpetrate on our family name.

Pantaloon   Just a minute, I wouldn't say 'grievous wrong' after all, there was a previous contract . . .

Dr Lombardi   Stop. I know exactly what you are about to say. It appeared, in fact, that the contract with the Turinese was binding a priori. Where as, of course, with greater reflection you realise ours takes precedence by its actual ratification by the tendering of the good lady's hand.

Pantaloon   Yes, but . . .

Dr Lombardi   And as you'd say so yourself, *concensus et non conubitus, facit virum.*

Pantaloon   Look, in plain English . . .

Dr Lombardi   *Ipso facto*, The lady is not for burning. As they say.

Pantaloon   Have you finished?

Dr Lombardi   Yes. Completely. And utterly.

Pantaloon   If you'll allow me to speak . . .

Dr Lombardi   Be my guest.

Pantaloon   Look, I am fully aware of your extensive legal knowledge . . .

Dr Lombardi   Of course, we'd turn a blind eye to the matter of the dowry, you understand. What's a few ducats here and there between friends, eh?

Pantaloon   What do I have to do to get a word in edgeways?

Dr Lombardi   There's no need to take umbrage, sir.

Pantaloon   With the greatest respect. Stuff your legal acumen, sir, there is nothing else I can do.

Dr Lombardi   You mean you are going through with this treacherous arrangement!

Pantaloon   Sir, I had given my word. And now my daughter has agreed to the whole thing – so as much as it pains me – I'm afraid there's nothing I can do. I was just about to come to explain to you and poor Silvio how dreadfully sorry I am for the whole horrid business.

Dr Lombardi   I can't exactly say that I'm surprised at that little minx of daughter, sir, but I am dumbfounded by your dispicable treatment of me. If you hadn't cast-iron concrete proof that that Rasponi was six feet under you should never have given the slightest glimmer of a hope to my son. Well, let me tell you, sir, you've made the arrangement and you should go through with it whatever the cost. Surely the news that he was dead is ample proof for the fellow to withdraw with his name intact. *Coram testibus*, sir, *coram testibus*. Infact, sir, I should simply insist that this arrangement be annulled and Clarice married instantly to my son, but I'd be ashamed to have such a hussy in my household. The daughter of a man who goes back on his word, sir, is no daughter at all. You have not merely injured me, but you have cruelly maimed the whole house of Lombardi. A plague be upon you. You'll live to regret this: *Omnia tempus habent.* Yes, you heard, *omnia tempus habent.*

Scene Two

Pantaloon   Go and fry in hell you overeducated stoat. The wart on the end of my arse is worth more than the entire house of Lombardi. It's not every day you get the chance of a son-in-law so well connected. And cultured. And rich. So stuff you and your petulant little offspring. The marriage has to be.

Enter **Silvio**.

Silvio   Your humble servant, Mr Pantaloon, sir.

Pantaloon   Ah. Good day, sir. (*Aside.*) There's steam coming out of his ears.

Silvio   I couldn't help but overhear, sir, that the marriage to Rasponi still stands. Is that correct?

Pantaloon   Well, I'm afraid it is, sir. Signed, sealed and delivered.

Silvio   Then, sir, you are no man of honour and no gentleman at all.

Pantaloon   I beg your pardon. How dare you insult a man of my standing.

Silvio   I don't care who I insult just count yourself lucky I haven't run you through.

Pantaloon   Don't dare threaten me in my own house.

Silvio   Well, come outside, if you are a man of honour.

Pantaloon   I demand to be treated with the respect and decorum I am due.

Silvio   Very well. You are a villian, a coward and a scavenging dog, sir.

Pantaloon   That's it, you ignorant little frog.

Silvio   I swear to heaven . . .

Silvio *grabs his sword.*

Pantaloon   Help! Help!

Scene Three

Enter **Beatrice**, *with sword drawn.*

Beatrice   Ha. I come in your defence.

Pantaloon   My dear son. Thank the heavens.

Silvio   The very man I wish to fight.

Beatrice (*aside*)   Oh, blast.

Silvio   Come, sir.

Pantaloon   Careful, son. He's as high as a kite.

Beatrice   I am no novice in the arts of fighting, sir. Do your worst. I fear nobody.

Pantaloon   Help! Help! Anyone!

Scene Four

Pantaloon *rushes towards the street.* **Beatrice** *and* **Silvio** *fight.* **Silvio** *falls and drops his sword.* **Beatrice** *stands over him, her sword pointing at his chest.*

Enter **Clarice**.

Clarice   Oh God. Please stop.

Beatrice   Beautiful Clarice, for you alone will I spare him, but in return you will remember your promise.

Exit **Beatrice**.

Clarice   Are you hurt, my love?

Silvio   'My love'? First you scorn me then you call me 'my love'. You perfidious wretch. You cankerous mould. How can you bear to humiliate me like this?

Clarice   No, Silvio. You don't understand. I love you, I adore you, you have my absolute fidelity.

Silvio   Fidelity! Is this your idea of fidelity? Marrying that bloodthirsty beast?

Clarice   But I haven't yet and I never will. I'd rather die than desert you.

Silvio   But you've only just now given your promise.

Clarice   No, the promise is not to marry him.

Silvio   So what exactly is this promise?

Clarice   I can't tell you.

Silvio   Why not?

Clarice   Because it's a promise.

Silvio   This just proves your guilt.

Clarice   No it doesn't. I'm completely innocent.

Silvio   If you're so completely innocent, then why don't you tell me?

Clarice   Because if I told you then I'd be guilty.

Silvio   Oh, for God's sake, at least tell me to whom you have sworn the promise.

Clarice   Federigo.

Silvio   Federigo. Well, that explains it.

Clarice   If I don't keep my word, then I am a liar.

Silvio   And you have the audacity to stand there and tell me you don't love him. You liar, you treacherous whore. Get out of my sight.

Clarice   If I didn't love you, why would I come running to save your life?

Silvio   But what is my life worth when it is weighed by such a miserable wretch?

Clarice   I love you with all my heart.

Silvio   I hate you with all my soul.

Clarice   I'll die if you don't believe me.

Silvio   I would sooner see you dead than unfaithful.

Clarice   Then you shall have that satisfaction.

Clarice *picks up his sword.*

Silvio   Go ahead. You'll be doing me a favour.

Clarice   How can you be so cruel?

Silvio   I have had the finest teacher.

Clarice   Then you want me dead?

Silvio   I don't know what I want any more.

Clarice   Oh but I do.

Clarice *turns the point against her breast.*

Scene Five

Enter **Smeraldina**.

Smeraldina (*to* **Clarice**)   What on earth do you think you're doing? (*To* **Silvio**.) And what are you doing standing there? Oh I expect you're having a whale of a time, aren't you, beautiful young women sacrificing themselves over you left, right and centre. Well, if he doesn't want you, miss, stuff him. Just tell him to go to hell. There's plenty more fish in the sea.

She throws down the sword. **Silvio** *picks it up.*

Clarice   You monstrous wretch. Is my death not even worth a single sigh? Well, I shall die, sir, of sorrow. I shall die and you shall have your satisfaction. And when it's all too late you'll realise my innocence and you will weep boiling tears for what you killed through your own barbarous cruelty.

Clarice *leaves.*

Smeraldina   I hope you're very pleased with yourself. She's on the brink of suicide and you just stood there like a stale panattone.

Silvio   Absolute nonsense. You don't really think she would have done it, do you?

Smeraldina   If it wasn't for me, mate, she'd already be dead.

Silvio   It was nowhere near her heart.

Smeraldina   You ignorant pig.

Silvio   See. You women are all hysterics.

Smeraldina   Hysterics! Listen, the only reason we get all the stick is because we haven't got a dick. Oh yes, a woman's hysterical but a bloke is full of passion, whereas I'd be called a slut you'd be a Jack the lad. Well, let me tell you, the only reason you get to run round like the cock of the midden is because of the unequal economic relations of the sexes, matey. If women had a position in this society that was equal to their tact, intelligence and ability to get things done you don't think they'd put up with you poncing round like some superannuated gondolier. They wouldn't give you a second glance, 'big boy'.

She leaves.

Scene Six

Silvio   You think you can fool me with that ridiculous display of mendacity. You traitorous strumpet. You perfidious whore. Even if he kills me in the trying, I'm going to find that notorious little Rasponi shit and the faithless Clarice shall watch him wallow in his own suppurating blood.

Exit **Silvio**.

Scene Seven

Truffaldino   Just my luck. Two gaffers and neither one of the beggars comes back for their scran, and I've been stood here like an escapee from the catacombs for two bloody hours. The next thing you know they'll both show up and I'll be up the Po without a paddle with terminal malnutrition. Oh hang on. Talk of the devil.

Florindo   Well, did you find that fellow, Pasqual?

Truffaldino   Funnily enough, not yet. I thought I was going to look for him after lunch?

Florindo   I've got no time to waste, it's imperative I get to him as soon as is humanly possible.

Truffaldino   Sir, it's 'imporative' that I get to some lunch as soon as is humanly possible or I'm going to pass away. If we don't order now all will be lost, sir.

Florindo   I'm not even hungry. Look, I'll go back to the post office myself and see what I can find out.

Truffaldino   Just a little bit of advice, sir, here in Venice it's advisable to eat at every mealtime or you can do yourself a mischief. It's the water, you know.

Florindo   What on earth are you on about? I really have to go, if I'm back for dinner, all well and good, if not then we'll just have to eat this evening.

Truffaldino   This evening!?

Florindo   Look, grab something to put you off if you're that desperate. Take this money, it's far too heavy to be trailing round. Put it in my trunk, here's the key.

Truffaldino   On the double, sir. Two ticks and I'll be back down with it.

Florindo   No, no. You hold on to it. I'm going right away. If I don't turn up for dinner then find me in the piazza. I'm going to find this Pasqual if it kills me.

Exit **Florindo**.

Scene Eight

Truffaldino   Thank God for that. If he wants to starve himself senseless that's his pigeon, but I tell you what, I'm buggered if I'm going on a diet for the sake of Pasqual.

Enter **Beatrice**.

Beatrice   Truffaldino.

Truffaldino   Oh my giddy aunt.

Beatrice   Truffaldino, did Mr Pantaloon Parsimoni give you a purse of a hundred ducats.

Truffaldino   Yes, sir, indeed he did.

Beatrice   Then why haven't you given them to me?

Truffaldino   Ah. Was it meant for you, your honour?

Beatrice   Was it meant for me? Well, what did he say when he gave it to you?

Truffaldino   I'm not sure. I think he said give it to your master.

Beatrice   And who is your master?

Truffaldino   You are.

Beatrice   Well, why on earth are you asking such ridiculous questions ?

Truffaldino   Just checking, sir. Can't be too careful.

Beatrice   Well, where is it?

Truffaldino   Where is what, sir?

Beatrice   The bag of ducats.

Truffaldino   I haven't a clue, sir.

Beatrice   What is that then?

Truffaldino   Oh, here it is, sir.

Beatrice   Is it all there?

Truffaldino   Of course it's all there. As if I would mess about with it.

Beatrice   I'm going to count this later.

Truffaldino (*aside*)   So what if it wasn't his. He's never going to notice.

Beatrice   Is that innkeeper about?

Truffaldino   He most certainly is, sir.

Beatrice   Tell him I have a friend joining me for dinner, so he'll need to lay on an extra few dishes.

Truffaldino   What do you mean? An extra few dishes?

Beatrice   I don't know. It's for Mr Pantaloon. I don't think he's much of an eater. I'd say we'd get away with four or five between us, as long as they're tasty.

Truffaldino   Leave it to me, guv.

Beatrice   See what you can do. I'm going to fetch Pantaloon from around the corner, just see that it's all sorted when I get back.

Truffaldino   No problem at all, sir.

Beatrice   Put this paper in my trunk. And be extremely careful with it, it's a bill of exchange for four thousand crowns.

Truffaldino   Rest assured, sir, I will give it singular attention.

Beatrice   Just make sure everything's ready.

Scene Nine

Truffaldino   Right, now this is a great chance to demonstrate my various skills at the ordering of a dinner. I'll just pop the paper . . . oh, bugger the paper, I'll sort it out later. More important matters. Hello. Garçon. Anybody there? Can you please advise Monsewer Brighella that I would like to speak to him toot sweet. Now the secret of a proper dinner is not simply in the selection, but the way it's all laid out. It's your presentation, isn't it.

Enter **Brighella**.

Brighella   Can I be of assistance?

Truffaldino   Indeed you can, my good man. My master is entertaining a very good friend of his and requests you prepare an enormous amount of food for them to eat of, immediately. I trust you have the necessaries on hand in the old kitchen, sir.

Brighella   Oh I always have the necessaries.

Truffaldino   So what would you recommend, then?

Brighella   For two people. A couple of courses maybe four little dishes each.

Truffaldino   Well, just throw a few more in just to be on the safe side.

Brighella   For the first course we have some nice soup, some whitebait, a meat platter and a fricandeau.

Truffaldino   I beg your pardon.

Brighella   A fricandeau. It's French. A sort of ragoût.

Truffaldino   Sounds just the ticket. But be careful with that frigandoo.

Brighella   Then we could do you a roast, a nice salad, a game pie and then follow it all up with a spotted dick.

Truffaldino   There's no need for that, sir. My master is a man of some standing.

Brighella   It's an English dish, sir.

Truffaldino   I don't care where it's from, sir, a dick's a dick in my book. I think we'll have a trifle. Very good. So how will the dishes be laid out, if you please?

Brighella   Well, the waiter will just bring them to the table.

Truffaldino   Ha, ha! That's where you are wrong. No, my friend, the laying of a table is a very special matter, believe me, sir, I am a stickler for the presentation.

Brighella   Well, the soup goes here, the whitebait, here. And there the cold cuts and we'll put the ragoût over there. OK?

Truffaldino   The 'fricandeau'?

Brighella   The fricandeau.

Truffaldino   What about something in the middle?

Brighella   Then you'd need an extra dish, wouldn't you?

Truffaldino   What do you think I am? A skinflint. We're talking about the laying out of a meal, sir. Do an extra dish, for God's sake.

Brighella   Maybe we could do a nice dip for the whitebait?

Truffaldino   A dip. Don't be so ridiculous. Where would the soup go.

Brighella   We could put the soup on one side and the dip on the other.

Truffaldino   No we could not, sir. This is an absolute outrage. You might know how to cook a pimpled dick, sir, but you don't have the first idea how to lay a table. Now, if this is your table, your five dishes must be placed like so, with your soup in the centre.

He tears a bit off the bill of exchange and puts it one one side.

And on the opposite side. The whitebait.

He tears another bit off.

Your sauce. Or 'dip' as you call it, would, of course, go here.

More tearing, etc.

And, here, we'd have the what-do-you-call-it.

Brighella   The fricandeau.

Truffaldino   And bob's your uncle.

Brighella   But isn't the dip too far away from the whitebait?

Truffaldino   Well, move them closer together then. For God's sake.

Scene Ten

Enter **Beatrice** *and* **Pantaloon**.

Beatrice   Excuse me. What are you doing?

Truffaldino   Ah, just a bit of culinary experimentation.

Beatrice   But isn't that my bill of exchange?

Truffaldino   Indeed it is, sir, and we'll have it stuck back together in no time.

Beatrice   You asinine twit. What on earth were you thinking of?

Pantaloon   Look, there's no harm done, I'll write you out another one.

Beatrice   That's not the point. What if it had been irreplaceable? You cretinous halfwit.

Truffaldino   Now hang on a minute, sir. None of this would have happened if he knew how to lay a table.

Brighella   Listen, I've been laying tables all my life.

Truffaldino   Look, don't try and tell your granny how to suck eggs, matey.

Beatrice (*to* **Truffaldino**)   Bugger off, you stupid little man.

Truffaldino   But it's a very important matter . . .

Beatrice   I'm warning you. Go. Away.

Truffaldino   Well, don't blame me if you have to stretch for your dip.

Exit **Truffaldino**.

Brighella   I can't make any sense of him. One minute he's as sharp as a whip, the next he's thick as a baron of beef, sir.

Beatrice   Don't worry about it. The attributes of intelligence are all put on. May we have dinner now?

Brighella   It might take some time if you're wanting five dishes for each course.

Pantaloon   Five dishes. Courses? Listen, a bit of risotto and a few leaves of lettuce will do me fine.

Beatrice   Yes. Whatever he fancies.

Pantaloon   And a couple of rissoles.

Brighella   Coming right up. If you'd like to make yourselves comfortable in your room, sir – lunch will be served in no time at all.

Beatrice   And tell Truffaldino to come and wait on us.

Brighella   It's your funeral, sir.

Scene Eleven

Beatrice, **Pantaloon**, **Waiters** *and* **Truffaldino**.

Beatrice   I hope you don't mind such a meagre meal.

Pantaloon   On the contrary, my dear sir, you are going to far too much trouble. You should be dining at my house, not me prevailing on you. It's just with Clarice at home I think it's more appropriate to keep you two apart till the knot's tied. Anyway, I'm very much obliged for your valiant bravery before, sir.

Beatrice   At least there was no blood spilt.

The **Waiters** *go through to the room* **Brighella** *had indicated, carrying wine, glasses, etc.*

Pantaloon   They're very efficient, aren't they?

Beatrice   This Brighella is a first-rate fellow. Used to serve a gentleman in Turin and I can tell you he hasn't changed his spots.

Pantaloon   There's an excellent little place the other side of the Rialto, you know. Often pop down there with a few friends. You can have quite a feast just sharing a couple of starters. They do a bloody good burgundy, if you'll pardon the French. Very fine indeed.

Beatrice   Yes, to eat in company is one of life's great pleasures. I dare say you have often seen good times, sir.

Pantaloon   And will see many more. I hope.

Truffaldino (*carrying a tureen of soup*)   Dinner is served. If you'd be so kind to take your seats, gents.

Beatrice   For God's sake, just put the soup down on the table.

Truffaldino   At your service, sir.

Pantaloon   He's a queer fish that fellow of yours. You don't think he's er . . . You know?

Beatrice   I beg your pardon?

Pantaloon   Let's go through, eh?

Beatrice (*to* **Truffaldino**)   Less of the acrobatics and a bit more concentration, please.

Truffaldino   Call this a dinner? One dish at a time? I tell you, you don't get much for your ducat in here. Let's a have a taster.

He tries it with a spoon he keeps in his trousers.

Always keep your tools handy. Not bad, actually.

He exits into the room.

Scene Twelve

First Waiter *carrying a dish, then* **Truffaldino**.

First Waiter   When is that tosser coming for the rest?

Truffaldino   Hold your horses. What's this then?

First Waiter   That's your charcuterie.

Truffaldino   I beg your pardon.

First Waiter   Your meat plate, mate. I'll get the next.

Exits.

Truffaldino   Mmm? What's this? Horse meat? Actually, not bad. A nice bit of brisket, that is. Mmm.

Enter **Florindo**.

Florindo   Where are you going with that?

Truffaldino   What, sir?

Florindo   That plate.

Truffaldino   The charcuterie, sir? I was just going to put it on the table.

Florindo   Who for?

Truffaldino   You, sir.

Florindo   But I wasn't even back.

Truffaldino   Ah, always thinking ahead, sir.

Florindo   But what's the idea of starting with the meat before the soup?

Truffaldino   It's an old Venetian custom, sir.

Florindo   It's absolute poppycock. Take it back to the kitchen. I will not have my meat previous to any other course.

Truffaldino   Yes, sir. Very good, sir.

Florindo   I just want to eat something quickly and lie down.

Truffaldino   On the double, sir.

Florindo   Will I ever find Beatrice?

He leaves.

As soon as **Florindo** *has disappeared into the other room,* **Truffaldino** *rushes into* **Beatrice**'s *room with the plate.*

First Waiter   For crying out loud. Oi Speedy Gonzales.

Truffaldino Coming. Quickly go and lay the table in there. That other fellow is screaming for soup.

First Waiter All right, wind your neck in.

He exits.

Truffaldino And what have we got here, then. The flickflack?

He tries some.

Absolutely delicious.

He exits to **Beatrice**'s *room.*

The **Waiters** *go through with the things for* **Florindo**.

Truffaldino Very good, lads. Quick as a rat in a priest's cassock this lot. Right. Two masters, two tables, one very handsome servant. And away we go. If I manage this lot I want a bloody medal never mind a ducat a day.

The **Waiters** *come out of* **Florindo**'s *room and head for the kitchen.*

Truffaldino Come on, hurry up with that soup, will you?

First Waiter Look, you worry about that table, we'll see to this one, OK?

He exits.

Truffaldino Cheeky little bastard.

First Waiter *comes back with the soup.*

Truffaldino Thank you. I'll deal with that. Go and get the rest of the stuff for room one.

He exits.

First Waiter If you want to run around like a blue-arsed fly, that's all right with me, mate, as long as I get the same tips as usual.

Truffaldino *comes out of* **Florindo**'s *room.*

Beatrice   Truffaldino

First Waiter   Hey, look lively.

Truffaldino   Just coming.

Truffaldino *goes into* **Beatrice***'s room.*

Second Waiter *brings in the boiled meat for* **Florindo***.*

First Waiter   Give me that here.

First Waiter *takes it,* **Second Waiter** *goes off.*

Truffaldino *appears with a pile of dirty plates.*

Florindo   Truffaldino.

Truffaldino   Give that to me. (*He wants to take the dish from* **First Waiter**.)

First Waiter   No, I'm taking this.

Truffaldino   Listen, he's shouting for me. (*Takes dish into* **Florindo**.)

First Waiter   Who the hell does he think he is?

Second Waiter *brings in a dish of rissoles, gives it to the* **First Waiter** *and leaves.*

First Waiter   I'm not taking it just to get screamed at.

Truffaldino *comes out of* **Florindo***'s room with dirty plates.*

First Waiter   Oi, Sancho Panza. Rissoles.

Truffaldino   Don't start.

First Waiter   Your rissoles.

First Waiter *leaves.*

Truffaldino   Who the hell would order rissoles? I could just take potluck, but then if they got eaten by a non-rissole orderer and the rissole orderer called for the rissoles that were ordered but went astray then I'd be right up the rissole. I know. Genius. I'll cut the rissoles in half and each room will have rissoles ordered or not. Four and four and one. Mmm. Who's that going to go to? Fair's fair, no favouritisation. (*He eats the spare rissole.*) Right. Rissoles away.

Enter **First Waiter** *carrying a pudding.*

First Waiter   Truffaldino. Your spotted dick.

Truffaldino   One moment.

Truffaldino *runs into* **Florindo**'s *room with a plate of rissoles.*

First Waiter   But the rissoles were for that room.

Truffaldino   Look, mind your own business. As they were so delicious the rissoles were shared around as a courtesy of one gentleman to another. You can't be too free with your rissoles.

First Waiter   Well, it's perfectly possible that they can all dine together, you know.

Truffaldino   What the hell's this?

First Waiter   Spotted dick.

Truffaldino   Who's it for?

First Waiter   Your master.

Truffaldino   But I ordered trifle.

First Waiter   Look, it's got nothing to do with me.

First Waiter *leaves it with* **Truffaldino**.

Truffaldino   It can't really be dick, can it.

He tastes some with great trepidation.

Very tasty, actually.

Beatrice   Truffaldino.

Truffaldino (*mouthful*)   I'll be right with you.

Florindo   Truffaldino.

Truffaldino (*stuffing more into his mouth*)   Bugger.

Enter **Beatrice**. *She sees* **Truffaldino** *eating*.

Beatrice   Stop that at once. Come in here and wait this table.

Exits into room one.

Truffaldino *puts the plate on the floor and goes into* **Beatrice**'s *room. Enter* **Florindo** *from his room.*

Florindo   Truffaldino. Where the devil's he got to?

Enter **Truffaldino** *from* **Beatrice**'s *room. Sees* **Florindo**.

Truffaldino   Here.

Florindo   Where did you disappear to?

Truffaldino   More dishes, sir.

Florindo   More food?

Truffaldino   Just a mo.

Florindo   Well, get a move on. I want to take this nap.

Truffaldino   Don't worry. Garçon. Is there anything else coming? (*Of the pudding.*) I'll keep this for later. (*Hides pudding.*)

Enter **First Waiter**.

First Waiter   Roast.

Truffaldino   Thank you. Now fruit. Fruit.

First Waiter   Calm down.

He exits.

Truffaldino   Eeny Meeny Miney Mo. (*Takes the roast to* **Florindo**'s *room.*)

Enter **First Waiter** *with the fruit bowl.*

First Waiter   Fruit. Where are you?

Enter **Truffaldino** *from* **Florindo**'s *room.*

Truffaldino   Thank you.

First Waiter   Anything else, your Lordship?

Truffaldino   Stay there. (*Takes fruit into* **Beatrice***'s room.*)

First Waiter   Look at him go.

Truffaldino (*re-emerging*)   No, that's it now. Everybody's happy.

First Waiter   Glad to hear it.

Truffaldino   All we want is a table for me.

First Waiter   Charming.

He leaves.

Truffaldino   Now for me pudding. There you go: two masters, three diners, four courses in all. Everybody's happy. Nobody's any the wiser. I have served to two, now I will eat for four. Thank you.

Scene Thirteen

The street outside **Brighella***'s inn.*

Smeraldina   Charming this. Sending me out at all hours to run messages to a common tavern. I can't make head nor tail of it. One minute she's going to top herself, the next she's sending secret letters to all and sundry. Well, I'm buggered if I'm setting foot in this fetid dump.

First Waiter *comes out.*

First Waiter   Hello, hello, hello. What can I do you for?

Smeraldina (*unimpressed*)   For Christ's sake. (*To him.*) Is there a Federigo Rasponi in residence?

First Waiter   Certainly is. Just finishing his meal.

Smeraldina   Well, is it possible I could have a word. I have something for him.

First Waiter   No problem, gorgeous. Want to come in?

Smeraldina   To that rat-hole. Listen, I'm a Lady's maid, you know.

First Waiter   Come on. You don't expect me to send him out here, do you? Anyway, he's currently engaged with Mr Parsimoni.

Smeraldina   I'm staying put.

First Waiter   Look. I'll send his servant out then.

Smeraldina   The little funny-looking fella?

First Waiter   That's the one.

Smeraldina   Top idea, mate.

First Waiter   Too shy to come in, are you? But you'll talk to any Tom, Dick and Harry on the street corner. I know your type.

First Waiter *exits*.

Smeraldina (*to herself*)   Wanker.

Scene Fourteen

Enter **Truffaldino**, *bottle, glass and napkin*.

Truffaldino   Did somebody call?

Smeraldina   It was me. I'm so sorry to drag you out.

Truffaldino   No trouble at all, miss. At your service.

Smeraldina   I hope I didn't disturb your dinner.

Truffaldino   Not to worry. It won't run away.

Smeraldina   No. Seriously.

Truffaldino   To be quite honest, I've bloody well stuffed meself, and your lovely eyes, miss, are a perfect digestif.

Smeraldina (*aside*)   He's quite sophisticated.

Truffaldino   Oh, yes. (*Burps.*) Hang on a mo, and I'll just go and relieve myself of my accoutrements and be back in a tick.

Smeraldina (*impressed*)   Accoutrements! (*To* **Truffaldino**.) My mistress has sent this letter to Mr Rasponi, and as it wouldn't exactly be decent for a young lady as myself to be seen in an inn on her own. I thought you might deliver it for me.

Truffaldino   It'd be an absolute pleasure. But first, madam, I must deliver a message to you.

Smeraldina   Who from?

Truffaldino   A very distinguished fellow, madam. Are you aquainted with a certain Truffaldino Battocchio?

Smeraldina (*aside*)   Truffaldino Battachio. (*To* **Truffaldino**.) Never heard of him.

Truffaldino   A very handsome fella, if you don't mind me saying so, short, very muscular, a fine turn of phrase and an expert at the laying of tables.

Smeraldina   Well, I don't know anyone of that description.

Truffaldino   Well, he loves you with all his heart.

Smeraldina   You're joking.

Truffaldino   Not at all. If there was any hope that his affections might be reciprocated he would reveal himself to you. I mean make himself known.

Smeraldina   Well, if I had some idea what he looked like, you never know. Maybe I'd fancy him.

Truffaldino   Shall I introduce you, then?

Smeraldina   If you want.

Truffaldino *goes out. Then returns, makes a bow, heaves a sigh and goes back out. Re-enter* **Truffaldino**.

Truffaldino   Did you see him?

Smeraldina   Who?

Truffaldino   The man totally besotted with your beauty.

Smeraldina   I only saw you.

Truffaldino   Oh.

Smeraldina   You're not besotted with my beauty, are you?

Truffaldino   Well, just a little bit.

Smeraldina   Why didn't you say so in the first place?

Truffaldino   I'm . . . rather shy.

Smeraldina (*aside*)   The little tinker.

Truffaldino   Well?

Smeraldina   Well, what?

Truffaldino   What do you say?

Smeraldina   I'm rather shy myself.

Truffaldino   Well, it's a perfect match, isn't it?

Smeraldina   Well, to tell you the truth. You're not bad. On the whole.

Truffaldino   Are you courting, miss?

Smeraldina   What sort of question's that?

Truffaldino   I suppose that means you are, then?

Smeraldina   On the contrary, it means I certainly am not.

Truffaldino   Hard as it may seem, neither am I.

Smeraldina   Of course I could have been married fifty times over, but I've never really met the right sort of man.

Truffaldino   What do you think of this sort of man?

Smeraldina   I don't know. We'd have to see.

Truffaldino   And if this sort of man wished to ask for your hand. How would he do that?

Smeraldina   You don't waste your time. Since both of my parents are dead if a man happened to be interested, I suppose he'd have to ask my master or my mistress.

Truffaldino   And what would they say?

Smeraldina   They'd say 'if it makes her happy'.

Truffaldino   And would it make you happy?

Smeraldina   Only if they were happy about it.

Truffaldino   Bloody hell, you need a degree in philosophy to get anywhere with you. Now give uz the letter and I'll bring you the answer and we'll have ourselves a nice little chinwag.

Smeraldina   OK.

Truffaldino   Have you got any idea what's in it?

Smeraldina   No. But I'm dying to find out.

Truffaldino   Look, I don't want to take him any insults or anything. I get it in the neck every time.

Smeraldina   I think it's a love letter.

Truffaldino   I'm in enough trouble as it is. If I don't know what's in it, I'm not taking it through.

Smeraldina   Couldn't we open it? We'd have to seal it back up though.

Truffaldino   Leave that to me. I know the perfect method. He'll be none the wiser.

Smeraldina   Go on then.

Truffaldino   Can you read?

Smeraldina   A bit. But you can, can't you?

Truffaldino   Well, to a point.

Smeraldina   Let's have a look.

Truffaldino   Now this is a very delicate operation. (*The letter gets torn.*)

Smeraldina   What are you doing!?

Truffaldino   Nothing. We'll soon put that right. There you go. (*It's open.*)

Smeraldina   Well, go on then.

Truffaldino   No. No. Ladies first.

Smeraldina (*looks at it*)   I can't make head nor tail of it.

Truffaldino (*looks at it*)   Me neither. Not a sausage.

Smeraldina   Well, what was the point of opening it?

Truffaldino   Hang on. Let's have another shot. Wait. Here's something.

Smeraldina   Yep. I think I can make out the odd letter.

Truffaldino   Well, let's go through the alphabet and work out which one it is. 'A'.

Smeraldina   That's not an 'A', it's an 'R'.

Truffaldino   Bloody hell they're quite similar, aren't they.

Smeraldina   'Ri, ri, ria.' No I don't think it's an 'R'. It's an 'M'. Mia.

Truffaldino   No, wait. It's 'Mio'. No wonder we can't read it. It's in bloody Italian.

Scene Fifteen

Enter **Beatrice** *and* **Pantaloon**.

Pantaloon   What are you doing here?

Smeraldina (*terrified*)   Nothing, sir. I was just on my way to find you.

Pantaloon   What do you want me for?

Smeraldina   My mistress was asking for you.

Beatrice   What's that you've got there?

Truffaldino   Nothing, sir. It's just a piece of paper.

Beatrice   Give me that here.

Truffaldino *hands her the piece of paper*.

Beatrice   What's this? This letter's addressed to me. Am I ever going to get a letter that hasn't been read by all and sundry.

Truffaldino   It was nothing to do with me.

Beatrice   Look, sir, a note from Lady Clarice warning me of Silvio's insane jealousy and this impudent rascal has the gall to go and open it.

Pantaloon (*to* **Smeraldina**)   And you, you had your grubby hands in this.

Smeraldina   I don't know anything about it, sir.

Beatrice   Well, who opened the letter?

Truffaldino   Not me.

Smeraldina   Not me.

Pantaloon   Well, who the devil brought it?

Smeraldina   Truffaldino. He was taking it to his master.

Beatrice   Is this true?

Truffaldino   Yes. I got it from Smeraldina.

Smeraldina   You little shit.

Pantaloon   You meddling hussy. I knew you'd be at the bottom of this. I've got a good mind to smack your backside.

Smeraldina   I beg your pardon. I have never been 'smacked' by any man, sir. I am outraged.

Pantaloon   'Outraged' are you?

Smeraldina   I'm not standing for this, you rheumatic old git. Goodbye.

Exit **Smeraldina**.

Pantaloon   Rheumatic old git!

Exit **Pantaloon** *in pursuit*.

Scene Sixteen

Beatrice, **Truffaldino**.

Truffaldino   Well, that's another fine mess I've got myself into.

Beatrice (*aside*)   Poor Clarice despairing over Silvio's jealousy. I'll have to uncover myself and put an end to this lunacy.

Truffaldino   I think I better make myself scarce.

Beatrice   Where do you think you're going?

Truffaldino   Nowhere.

Beatrice   Why did you open this letter?

Truffaldino   It was Smeraldina. I had absolutely nothing to do with it.

Beatrice   Smeraldina. This is the second letter today. Come here.

Truffaldino   Have mercy on me, sir.

Beatrice   Here.

Truffaldino   Please, I didn't mean it, sir.

Beatrice *gives him a good thrashing*.

Florindo *appears at the window.*

Florindo   Beat my man, would you?

Truffaldino   Please, stop. Ow.

Beatrice   Never, never open my letters again.

Scene Seventeen

Beatrice *leaves.*

Truffaldino   Thank you. Thank you very much. After everything I've done for that bastard. If you're not happy with your service sack me by all means, but there's no need to go for grievous bodily harm.

Enter **Florindo**.

Florindo   What's that you're saying?

Truffaldino   Oh nothing, sir. Just that beating other people's servants is a disgrace and insult to their master, sir.

Florindo   It is a heinous insult. Who was that man?

Truffaldino   I don't know, sir. I haven't seen him before in my life.

Florindo   This isn't funny. What on earth did he beat you for?

Truffaldino   Really, I don't know. It must have been because I spat on his shoe, sir.

Florindo   Spat on his shoe?

Truffaldino   By mistake, sir.

Florindo   You blithering idiot. Didn't you think to defend yourself. I suppose you thought it was funny to lay your own master open to an insult. Have you any idea how serious that could be. Well, if you like a good thrashing now and again, I'd be happy to oblige.

Florindo *beats* **Truffaldino** *and leaves.*

Truffaldino   Well, that's it. I definitely know I've got two masters now, as I've had my wages from each one. I mean two. Or . . . ? Oh, sod it. 'The interval.'

Interval.

Act Three

Scene One

A room in the inn. Enter **Truffaldino**.

Truffaldino (*burps*)   To be quite honest it was worth having two beatings to get two excellent meals. Supper number one was absolutely first class but supper number two was in a second first class all of its own. Bad times look a lot better on a full belly – I'll tell you that much. I'm going to keep this lark up as long as I can still waddle upright without need of assistance. Righty-ho. What's on the agenda? Numero uno is out on the town and numero duo's snoring like a babe in arms, so I reckon it's high time to get these clothes out. So we'll sort these trunks out and have a shufty through to see what's what. I'll need a hand. Garçon!

Enter two **Waiters**.

First Waiter   What?

Truffaldino   I just need a hand getting a couple of trunks out of those rooms here.

First Waiter (*to* **Second Waiter**)   That's your job, mate.

Truffaldino   Come on. I'll make it worth your while.

Truffaldino *goes out with the* **Second Waiter**.

First Waiter (*aside*)   There's a rabbit off somewhere. He seems a bit too keen for my liking.

Truffaldino *comes back*.

Truffaldino   Careful. Put it down here. (*They put a trunk down.*) Right. T'other one. But shh, the guvnor's having a kip.

First Waiter (*aside*)   He's definitely up to something. The servant of two masters. More like the thief of two masters.

Truffaldino (*coming from* **Florindo**'*s room with* **Second Waiter**) We'll put this one here. Champion. Right, you can piss off now, thank you very much.

First Waiter Yes, bugger off to the kitchen, like a good lad. (*To* **Truffaldino**, *who's struggling with a case*.) Can I help you at all?

Truffaldino No, thanks all the same. All under control.

First Waiter Fair enough, if you want to break your back that's your problem, smart-arse.

Exit **First Waiter**.

Truffaldino Thank God for that. A bit peace and quiet. (*Takes key from his pocket*.) Which one's this? Let's have a gander. (*Tries it in a trunk. It works*.) Yes, right first time. The Brain of Bergamot strikes again. I suggest that this key, therefore, will open this trunk over here. (*Tries it*.) He puts it in. He turns the key. Yes. Two in a row. There will be riots on the streets tonight. Right, let's be having you.

He takes the clothes out of both trunks; lays them on the table. In each trunk there must be a black jacket, books, papers and various other items.

Let's have a look in these pockets. You very often find the odd biscuit and the like.

He feels in the pocket of **Beatrice**'*s jacket and finds a small photo / miniature*

Look at that. Very nice. Now there's a handsome young fella. I'm sure I know him from somewhere. Who the hell is it? Hey, he looks the spit of my master, except with different clothes and wotnot.

Scene Two

Florindo (*off*)   Truffaldino.

Truffaldino   Oh bloody hell. I've woke the miserable sod up. If he comes out here I'm snookered with these two cases. Get this rubbish back in and deny everything. That's the ticket.

Florindo (*off*)   Truffaldino.

Truffaldino (*shouts*)   Here, sir. (*To himself.*) Shit. Where did this jacket come from?

Florindo (*off*)   Are you coming or do I have to come out there with a stick and get you?

Truffaldino   Coming at once, sir.

Truffaldino *throws everything in the trunks willy-nilly.*

Enter **Florindo** *in a dressing gown.*

Florindo   What the devil are you doing?

Truffaldino   I was just giving your clothes an airing like you asked, sir.

Florindo   Whose is that other trunk?

Truffaldino   What trunk? Oh. Haven't a clue, sir. I've only just noticed it.

Florindo   Give me my black jacket.

Truffaldino   No problem, sir.

He opens **Florindo**'s *trunk, takes out the black jacket. He helps* **Florindo** *try it on.* **Florindo** *finds the miniature.*

Florindo   What's this?

Truffaldino (*aside*)   Balls.

Florindo (*aside*)   There is no mistake. This is my picture. The one I gave to Beatrice. (*To* **Truffaldino**.) How did this get into my jacket pocket?

Truffaldino   Don't panic.

Florindo   Out with it. What is this picture doing in my jacket pocket?

Truffaldino   Please, please, forgive me, sir, but I have taken a great liberty. The picture infact is mine, sir, and I put it there for safekeeping.

Florindo   Safekeeping? How did you come by such a picture?

Truffaldino   I inherited it, sir. From my previous master.

Florindo   Inherited it!

Truffaldino   When he died I was left several things and flogged them all except this exquisite item, sir.

Florindo   When did your master die?

Truffaldino   A week ago. (*Aside.*) You do realise I'm making this up.

Florindo   What was his name?

Truffaldino   I do not know, sir, the man went incognito.

Florindo   Incognito. How long were you in his service?

Truffaldino   Not long at all. Maybe twelve days, sir.

Florindo (*aside*)   This is Beatrice. Fleeing Turin dressed as a man. Oh this is unbearable. (*To* **Truffaldino**.) Was he young, your master?

Truffaldino   Alas, a very young man, sir.

Florindo   Without a beard?

Truffaldino   Not even bumfluff, sir.

Florindo (*to himself*   It was Beatrice. No doubt about it. (*To* **Truffaldino**.) Do you at least know where this master was from?

Truffaldino   I'm trying to remember.

Florindo   Could it have possibly been Turin?

Truffaldino   Exactly. Turin. That's the one.

Florindo (*to himself*)   Every word is a dagger to my heart.
(*To* **Truffaldino**.) And you are certain the man is dead?

Truffaldino   As a dodo, sir. (*Aside.*) Think about it.

Florindo   What did he die of?

Truffaldino   He had a nasty accident and that was that.
(*Aside.*) A very good answer.

Florindo   So where was he buried?

Truffaldino (*aside*)   For crying out loud. (*To* **Florindo**.)
He wasn't buried. Another servant put him in a coffin and
sent him home.

Florindo   And this servant was the man for whom you
collected the letter at the post office.

Truffaldino   Yes. The very same, sir, the infamous
Pasqual.

Florindo   Then Beatrice is dead. The torture of the
journey must have broke her heart and killed her. Beatrice.
This is a living hell.

Florindo *leaves in tears*.

Scene Three

Truffaldino   What have I done now? Poor delicate soul.
It's as if he knew the gentleman in question. Weeping like a
child, and all I was doing was covering up for the bloody
trunks. Right, I'm getting these buggers (*the trunks*) out before
I get in any more trouble.

Enter **Beatrice**.

Beatrice   I assure you, Mr Pantaloon, there are some
definite discrepancies in these accounts. I'm sure the last
consignment of sun-dried tomatoes has been entered twice.

Pantaloon   Maybe my young men have made some
mistake. Don't worry, I'll have it gone through with a fine-
tooth comb.

Beatrice   Don't worry, I've a complete list of everything
copied into my record book with me, if we sit down with all
the figures we'll have it sorted out in no time. Truffaldino.

Truffaldino   Hello.

Beatrice   Have you the key to my trunk?

Truffaldino   Yes. Here you are, sir.

Beatrice   And what's it doing out there?

Truffaldino   I was just going to air your clothes, sir.

Beatrice   And whose is that other trunk?

Truffaldino   Haven't a clue, sir. It must belong to the
other geezer what's just arrived.

Beatrice   There is a notebook in my trunk. Can you
retrieve it for me so that I can sort out this matter with Mr
Pantaloon?

Truffaldino   No problem at all, sir. (*Aside.*) God preserve
me.

He opens the trunk and looks for the notebook.

Pantaloon   Of course, if there is any material discrepancy
the matter will be reconciled not withstanding, sir.

Beatrice   Just a tick, I've got it all written down.

Truffaldino   Is it this one?

Beatrice   It looks like it. (*Looks in it.*) What in hell's name
is this?

Truffaldino   Bollocks.

Beatrice (*aside*)   Here are two of the letters I wrote to Florindo. What's going on?

Pantaloon   Mr Federigo, are you feeling all right?

Beatrice   It will pass, I assure you. (*To* **Truffaldino**.) Truffaldino, how did these get into my trunk?

Truffaldino   I don't really know, sir.

Beatrice   Out with it. The truth, you lying toad.

Truffaldino   Please, sir, that is infact my own book, and I took the liberty of putting them in there myself, sir. Terribly sorry. (*Aside.*) If it worked once . . .

Beatrice   If it's your book how come you gave it to me?

Truffaldino (*aside*)   Clever bastard. (*To* **Beatrice**.) Sir, I haven't had it very long, sir – so it seemed unfamiliar.

Beatrice   So where did it come from?

Truffaldino   I was left it, sir, when my previous master sadly died, sir.

Beatrice   Died? When did this master die?

Truffaldino   Hard to say, sir. Twelve days ago?

Beatrice   But you were in Verona with me twelve days ago. That's exactly when I met you.

Truffaldino   Absolutely right, sir. I had to leave for Verona on account of the grief, sir.

Beatrice   And was this master called Florindo?

Truffaldino   I think he was, sir.

Beatrice   Florindo Aretusi?

Truffaldino   That's the fella.

Beatrice   And he is dead?

Truffaldino   As a door nail, sir.

Beatrice   Oh this is too much. How did he die? Where is he buried?

Truffaldino   He fell into a canal, knocked his head on a gondola, drowned of an instant and was never seen again, sir.

Beatrice   No. No. No. Florindo dead? My hope, my being, my life, my everything is gone. Love has vanished from the world. All my plans, my disguises, the danger, the suffering have all been for nothing. It was torture enough to lose a brother, but now a husband too? If I am the cause of this let heaven tear me limb from limb and rip my heart out of my body as it is useless to me now. Not tears, not medicine, not anything will ever bring it back to life. Florindo is dead. And I am dead with grief. I can't stand this light. I followed you in life, so I shall follow you in death, my dearest love.

She exits.

Pantaloon   Truffaldino!

Truffaldino   Mr Pantaloon, sir.

Pantaloon   A woman!

Truffaldino   And not bad at all if you don't mind me saying so.

Pantaloon   This is extraordinary.

Truffaldino   You can say that again.

Pantaloon   Extraordinary.

Truffaldino   Well, it's certainly a turn-up for the books.

Pantaloon   I must go straight home and tell my daughter.

Exit **Pantaloon**.

Truffaldino   So it's not the servant of two masters any more but the servant of one master and another-master-who-on-revealing-their-true-nature-appears-to-really-have-

been-quite-a-good-looking-mistress all along. Not as snappy,
is it?

Scene Four

Courtyard, **Pantaloon**'s *house.*

Enter **Dr Lombardi**.

Dr Lombardi   That doddering old clot's going to get it
this time. I shall brook the argument no further.

Enter **Pantaloon**.

Pantaloon   Ah, my dear Doctor, how very good to see
you.

Dr Lombardi   I'm surprised you even have the gall to
speak to me, sir.

Pantaloon   But I have some wonderful news.

Dr Lombardi   Don't tell me. They've married already. I
don't give a damn for your news, sir.

Pantaloon   Please, listen . . .

Dr Lombardi   Speak then, you villanous Turk.

Pantaloon (*aside*)   He's asking for it. (*To* **Dr Lombardi**.)
Sir, my daughter will marry your son, whenever you wish.

Dr Lombardi   Oh I am very much obliged, but don't put
yourself to any inconvenience, sir. I'm afraid it would turn
my son's stomach to even contemplate the matter, the man
from Turin is perfectly welcome to her.

Pantaloon   But the man from Turin is not a man from
Turin.

Dr Lomabardi   I don't care where he's from, sir, she can
take the blaggard whatever his provenance.

Pantaloon   But . . .

Dr Lombardi   And I don't want to hear anything further.

Pantaloon   Please, this is important.

Dr Lombardi   We'll see what's important.

Pantaloon   Please, my daughter's reputation is entirely untarnished.

Dr Lombardi   Go to the devil, sir.

Pantaloon   Go to the devil, yourself.

Dr Lombardi   You welching runt.

Pantaloon   I beg your pardon?

Dr Lombardi   I said welching, sir.

Dr Lombardi *storms off.*

Scene Five

Pantaloon   Sod you. The man's a rabid goat. Saints preserve us, here's another one.

Enter **Silvio**.

Silvio   Pantaloon. I would like to rip the innards from your overweight gut.

Pantaloon   Please, Mr Silvio, sir, I have some very good news for you.

Silvio   You malignant worm.

Pantaloon   I want you to know, sir, my daughter's marriage to Mr Federigo is off.

Silvio   Don't even try to make a fool of me.

Pantaloon   It's the God's honest truth. Please, you can have her, sir, she's yours for the taking.

Silvio   Oh thank the heavens. I am ressurrected.

Pantaloon   At least he's a little more civil than his father.

Silvio   But how can I knowingly accept a woman who has been wedded to another for so long?

Pantaloon   Because, sir, that other, that Federigo Rasponi, is no other than Beatrice his sister.

Silvio   I don't understand.

Pantaloon   Don't be an arse. The person we assumed was Federigo was his sister in disguise.

Silvio   Dressed as man?

Pantaloon   No, dressed as the Goddess Athena.

Silvio   Bloody hell. Now there's a turn-up.

Pantaloon   Believe me, no one was more surprised than me.

Silvio   How on earth did this come about?

Pantaloon   Let's go to my house. I haven't even had time to tell Clarice herself, you can hear the whole story together.

Silvio   Oh I must humbly apologise for anything I might have said, sir.

Pantaloon   Let's forget it. I'm quite familiar with the hot passions of love. You come along with me, son.

Exeunt.

Scene Six

Darkness. The inn. **Beatrice** *and* **Florindo** *come out of their rooms, each carrying a rope. Neither sees the other. Each has a picture of their loved ones. They both make careful preparations to hang themselves. They each kiss their picture and jump off the chair. [If this is not possible the method of suicide should need elaborate preparation and be painful to witness.]* **Brighella** *and the* **First Waiter** *come in with a lamp and accidentally see* **Beatrice** *jumping into oblivion.*

Brighella (*to* **First Waiter**)   And then I said to him . . .
(*On seeing* **Beatrice**.) Stop in the name of God.

They try to support her. She struggles. The **First Waiter** *tries to cut her down.*

Beatrice   Let me go. Let me die.

First Waiter   This is madness itself.

Florindo *then sees* **Beatrice**.

Florindo (*choking*)   Oh my God.

Beatrice   No one can stop me.

Suddenly **Brighella** *and* **First Waiter** *see* **Florindo**.

Beatrice   Florindo.

The **First Waiter** *has cut her down. They fall in a heap.*

Florindo   My Beatrice.

Beatrice   Alive?

Florindo *is choking.*

Florindo (*choking*)   My dearest love.

Beatrice   Florindo.

Brighella *gets up and rushes to assist* **Florindo**.

Brighella   What are you thinking of? You haven't paid
up yet.

They cut down **Florindo**. *He stands staring in astonishment at*
Beatrice. *She is equally dumbstruck.* **Brighella** *and the* **First
Waiter** *watch as* **Beatrice** *and* **Florindo** *are reunited.*

Florindo   Beatrice.

Beatrice   Florindo.

They kiss.

Scene Seven

Florindo   But what drove you to this madness?

Beatrice   News that you were dead.

Florindo   Who said I was dead?

Beatrice   My servant.

Florindo   And my servant told me that you too had passed away.

Beatrice   It was this book that caused me to believe him.

Florindo   But that book was in my trunk. What's going on? Of course, the very same way my picture got into my jacket pocket. The servants.

Beatrice   Those scheming little rascals. Lord knows what they've been up to.

Florindo   Where the hell are they? Let's sort this out once and for all. (*To* **Brighella**.) Where are our servants, sir?

Brighella   I'm afraid I have no idea, whatsoever, Would you like me to find them by any chance?

Florindo   Of course I want someone to find them. Have them grabbed by the scruff of the neck and dragged here at once.

Brighella   I'm afraid I've only ever seen one of them, but Charlie here will sort them out. Just a little word in your ear, sir, but it is customary to mention any suicides, maimings or sundry self-mutilation when you check in, sir, as all such activities are subject to a little service charge as they often result in us having to get in a cleaner. Nothing personal, you understand. Just something to bear in mind for the future, sir.

Exit **Brighella**.

Scene Eight

Florindo   So you came to Venice too?

Beatrice   I arrived this morning.

Florindo   But I arrived this morning too. How did we miss each other?

Beatrice   Fate has enjoyed tormenting us a little.

Florindo   But, Beatrice, is Federigo really dead?

Beatrice   You know he is. He died instantly.

Florindo   But I was told he was alive and well and here in Venice.

Beatrice   My dearest Florindo. It was me. I followed you using his name and clothing.

Florindo   Yes, yes, I know about the disguise from the letter your steward sent you.

Beatrice   From the letter my steward sent me?

Florindo   My servant gave it to me by mistake.

Beatrice   And you opened it?

Florindo   I had to. It had your name on it.

Beatrice   Exactly.

Florindo   Beatrice, the whole of Turin was buzzing with your flight. How can you go back there now.

Beatrice   Quite easily, as your 'wife'.

Florindo   But, sweetheart, I can never go back there. I am wanted for murder.

Beatrice   I've collected sufficient funds from Federigo's business ventures here in Venice to pay off whatever fine they throw at you. (You'd not believe what you can make out of sun-dried tomatoes.) Oh Florindo. I think everything is going to be all right, believe me. Where are those blessed servants?

Florindo   Look, here's one of them now.

Beatrice   Looking guilty if you ask me.

Scene Nine

Truffaldino *is frogmarched in between* **Brighella** *and the* **First Waiter**.

Florindo   Come on, here, there's nothing to be scared of.

Beatrice   We're not going to harm you.

Truffaldino (*aside*)   A likely story, I'm still recovering from the last lot.

Brighella   Well, that's one found. We'll soon have the other one.

Florindo   Excellent. We must have both blaggards together.

Brighella (*to* **First Waiter**)   You do know what he looks like, don't you?

First Waiter   I haven't a monkey's. He's the only one I've seen.

Brighella   Someone must have seen him.

Exit **Brighella**.

First Waiter   Listen, if he'd so much as put his nose round the door I'd've clocked him.

Exit **First Waiter**.

Florindo   Right. Now you can explain how this picture got in this pocket and how this book was miraculously switched around. And why you and the other rascal plotted to drive us into despair.

Truffaldino (*to* **Florindo**)   Please. I can explain
everything. May I just have a moment. It is all that will be
needed.

He draws **Florindo** *aside.*

I have to point out none of this is my fault, sir. It's all down
to that Pasqual, the lady's servant, sir. He twuddled all the
stuff up, and put it back without telling me anything about
it. And then he begged me and prayed and pleaded for me,
sir, to take the blame on myself on account of his deep
family troubles, sir, and since I am the sweetest and kind-
hearted soul, who'd have himself hung, drawn and
quartered rather than see another man in trouble, sir, I have
indeed kept you from the truth. Had I known the picture
was of you and you'd be caused such intolerable distress I
would immediately have had myself flogged. And that's the
God's honest truth, sir.

Beatrice   What on earth's going on?

Florindo   So the man who asked you to collect the letter
from the post office was Pasqual?

Truffaldino   Yes, the very man, sir.

Florindo   Why didn't you tell me this. You knew how
anxious I was to find this Pasqual.

Truffaldino   He begged me on his very life, sir, not to
give him away.

Florindo   But am I not your master?

Truffaldino   But I promised poor Pasqual, sir. To protect
him from a hiding.

Florindo   I've got a good mind to give you both a good
hiding.

Beatrice   What's going on?

Florindo   The fool was explaining that –

Truffaldino For the love of God above, please don't give poor Pasqual away. Say it was me, sir, beat me if you like, sir, but please save poor Pasqual from a pasting.

Florindo You're very loyal, aren't you.

Truffaldino I love him like a brother. Now let me go to the lady and take the blame, sir, no doubt she'll scold me as is her right, but you'll see I'll take it as a man of honour.

Florindo What a loyal and upright fellow you've turned out to be.

Truffaldino (*taking* **Beatrice** *to one side*) Sorry, madam.

Beatrice You were over there a very long time.

Truffaldino You see, the gentleman has a servant, a one Pasqual, ma'am. And a more dim-witted nonce you have never encountered. Having mixed all of his accoutrements up, he was sure to be expelled from service only to end up starving with him and his five children on the side of the road. And so, to get him out of this tight spot, I, quick as a flash, conjured the story of the book, the dead master who hit his head and was drowned and whatnot, in a desperate effort to save the man from penury, or worse. And thus I was allowing Mr Florindo to believe I was to blame.

Beatrice But why take the blame if you don't have to?

Truffaldino To save Pasqual, ma'am.

Florindo You're taking your time, aren't you.

Truffaldino Ma'am, please, I beg you, please don't let the man get into trouble.

Beatrice Which man?

Truffaldino Pasqual, ma'am.

Beatrice You and this Pasqual are a right pair of rascals.

Truffaldino But we share a common humanity, ma'am.

Florindo   For God's sake, Beatrice, let's put an end to this matter before it drags on into the new millennium, why don't we just forget about this as an 'expression of our current good fortune'.

Beatrice   But surely, your servant . . .

Truffaldino   Don't mention Pasqual.

Beatrice   You're right, but I ought to settle everything with Mr Parsimoni right away. Will you come with me?

Florindo   Of course, but I have an appointment here with my banker. Go on ahead and I'll join you presently.

Beatrice   I'll wait for you at Pantaloon's, and please, darling, don't be long.

Florindo   Wait a minute. I don't even know where he lives.

Truffaldino   Don't worry, I'll show you.

Beatrice   Very well, I'll just go and sort myself out then.

Truffaldino   Excellent. Don't worry, I'll be with you anon.

Beatrice   Oh Florindo. What torture I've been through because of you.

Exit **Beatrice**.

Scene Ten

Florindo   And mine was no less severe, my angel.

Truffaldino   Sir, I've realised without Pasqual Miss Beatrice has no one to help her get ready. Perhaps it's best to allow me to be at her service, sir?

Florindo   Yes, of course, an excellent observation, but only if she is served with exemplary diligence.

Truffaldino   Oh yes indeed, sir. She'll get double attention. A masterpiece of timing. The sheer effrontery, the pirouettes of logic, the fine balance of nuance. They are cheering in the gallery. This is the crowning and most astonishing of all Truffaldino's bravura performances. Can the man do anything wrong?

Florindo   How many strange things can happen in one day. Tears, anguish, sheer despair and yet in the end such resolution and incalcuable joy. When we move from pleasure to pain we miss our former state so keenly, but when our fortunes move the other way round, one feels as if there was never an unhappy moment in one's entire life.

Beatrice   I'm back. That was quick, wasn't it?

Florindo   I thought you were going to change those damn clothes?

Beatrice   I think they rather suit me.

Florindo   Please, darling, pop yourself into a blouse and bodice. You shouldn't hide your figure from me for a moment longer.

Beatrice   Nonsense, I'll wait for you at Pantaloon's, get Truffy to bring you there as soon as poss.

Florindo   Don't worry. If this banker doesn't show up soon, I'll just come along anyway.

Beatrice   Good, if you really love me you'll not waste a second.

Truffaldino   So you wish me to stay here with Mr Florindo?

Beatrice   Yes, show him over to Pantaloon's.

Truffaldino   What a good idea seeing as Pasqual is not here.

Beatrice   Do whatever he bids you to, I love him more than I love myself.

Beatrice *exits*.

Scene Eleven

Truffaldino   I can't believe he'd run off like that, just when his mistress needed to be dressed.

Florindo   I'm sorry?

Truffaldino   Pasqual. I swear I love his funny scrunched-up face and pity his terrible bad luck, but what a lazy little sod he's turned out to be. Where as I pride myself, sir, on doing the work of two men.

Florindo   Well, come and help me dress, will you. Sod the bloody banker.

Truffaldino   And then we'll nip over to Pantaloon's?

Florindo   Yes. What about it?

Truffaldino   Well, I hope it's not too much to ask, sir, but I hoped to ask you a favour.

Florindo   A favour. After everything you've put me through!

Truffaldino   I must ask you to remember, sir, that any trouble was Pasqual's doing not mine.

Florindo   But where is this blessed Pasqual? What is he? Invisible?

Truffaldino   He'll show up, the ungracious cad, and I'll put paid to him. But about this favour, sir.

Florindo   What is it?

Truffaldino   I am in love, sir.

Florindo   You?

Truffaldino   With a girl, sir, and she's a servant of Mr Parsimoni, sir.

Florindo   What on earth has any of this to do with me?

Truffaldino   I just hoped you could, put a word in, sir.

Florindo   Well, the girl mightn't even like you.

Truffaldino   Oh she wants me, sir, no mistake. All I ask is a kind word, sir. It'd make all the difference.

Florindo   But how could you afford a wife?

Truffaldino   Don't worry about that, sir, I'm very versatile. I'll get some advice from Pasqual.

Florindo   If I was you I'd ask someone with a little more sense.

Exit **Florindo**.

Truffaldino   Well, if I don't start having a bit of sense now, I think I never will.

Exit **Truffaldino** *(walking into a door)*.

Scene Twelve

A room in **Pantaloon**'s *house*.

Pantaloon   Come, dear Clarice, let bygones be bygones. You can see Silvio has repented and is begging for forgiveness. Admittedly the poor lad behaved a bit badly, et cetera, but it was all out of love. If I can forgive him for his little indiscretions, I'm sure you can, sweetpea.

Silvio   If what you have suffered, Clarice, is the tiniest measure of the torment I have felt, you'll know how the fear of losing you drove me to such mad despair. I love you more than life itself. Surely, heaven demands that we be happy. Please don't let revenge darken what should be the brightest day of our lives.

Dr Lombardi   I beseech you, my dear, dear daughter-in-law, try to understand the poor child. He was on the very brink of lunacy.

Smeraldina   Come on, miss, there's nothing to gain by moping round. All men are bastards to some degree or other. But you'll have to have one one day, so if you're forced to take your medicine, I'd get it over with.

Pantaloon You see. Smeraldina likens marriage to medicine. Not poison, dear. (*Aside.*) We have to try and cheer her up.

Dr Lomabardi Certainly. Marriage is a confection, a sherbet fountain, a bag of bonbons.

Silvio Clarice, not a word from your sweet lips. I know I am a wretch but at least punish me with words. This silence is too much for me. Look, I'm at your feet, please have mercy on me.

Clarice (*to* **Silvio**) Oh Silvio.

Pantaloon Did you hear? A sigh. A very good sign.

Dr Lombardi (*to* **Silvio**) Go on. Follow it up.

Smeraldina They reckon a sigh is like lightning, there's bound to be rain sooner or later.

Silvio If my blood could wash that wicked stain of cruelty from you, believe me, I would cut open these veins. But since it can't, let these tears wash away my mistakes.

Clarice *sighs again.*

Pantaloon Bravo!

Dr Lombardi Excellent. Excellent.

Pantaloon (*takes* **Silvio**'s *hand*) Up with you. (*Takes* **Clarice**'s.) You too. Now take each other's hands and make peace. We'll have no more tears, only love and laughter and happiness, let heaven bless you both.

They hold hands.

Dr Lombardi That's more like it.

Smeraldina They've done it. They've done it.

Silvio (*holding her hand*) My darling. I beg you.

Clarice   You ungrateful wretch.

Silvio   My darling.

Clarice   You uncircumcised dog.

Silvio   My sugarplum.

Clarice   You rat. You canker.

Silvio   My sweet angel.

Clarice   Ah! (*Sighs.*)

Pantaloon   Going, going . . .

Silvio   Forgive me. For the love of heaven.

Pantaloon   Gone.

Clarice   I forgive you.

Dr Lombardi   Thank the Lord that's over.

Smeraldina   The patient is prepared, give her her medicine.

Scene Thirteen

Enter **Brighella**.

Brighella   Ah, Mr Pantaloon, sir, hope I haven't come at a bad time.

Pantaloon   Quite the reverse, my good friend. It was you, was it not, who told me all those fine tales and assured me that this was Mr Federigo, did you not?

Brighella   My dear sir, who would not have been mistaken. Especially with young women these days.

Pantaloon   Whatever, whatever, what's done is done. Let us ask, instead, what is new?

Brighella   Well, the good Lady Beatrice is here to pay her respects, sir.

Pantaloon   Show her in. Show her in.

Clarice   Poor, poor Lady Beatrice. I am so delighted her troubles are over.

Pantaloon   You were sorry for her?

Clarice   Of course.

Silvio   But what about me?

Scene Fourteen

Enter **Beatrice**.

Beatrice   I have come to beg your forgiveness and implore you all to pardon the terrible confusion I have caused.

Clarice   Not another word, my friend. (*Embraces her.*)

Silvio   Hang on a minute.

Beatrice   What's wrong with her embracing another woman?

Silvio (*aside*)   It's the clothes.

Pantaloon   Well, I must say for such a young woman you certainly don't lack any get-up-and-go, do you?

Dr Lombardi   You've got rather too much, if you ask me.

Beatrice   Love can make us do extraordinary things.

Pantaloon   And you have found your young gentleman?

Beatrice   Yes, it seems that the heavens are smiling on us.

Dr Lombardi   I think you've gained yourself quite a reputation, young lady.

Beatrice   My reputation is no business of yours, sir.

Silvio   Father, please leave everyone to their own business and stop moralising. All I want now is that everyone in the world be as happy as I am. If they want to get married, let them all get married, for God's sake.

Smeraldina (*to* **Silvio**)   Well, infact, I'd like to get married, actually.

Silvio   Who the devil to?

Smeraldina   Anyone really.

Silvio   Well, go on then. Find somebody. I'll be here for you.

Clarice   Here for what?

Silvio   A dowry.

Clarice   A dowry!

Silvio (*aside*)   Charming, I see she's not going to give anyone else a nibble of her cake.

Scene Fifteen

Truffaldino   Hello there. Respects to the company.

Beatrice (*to* **Truffaldino**)   Where is Mr Florindo?

Truffaldino   He's awaiting downstairs for permission to come in.

Pantaloon   Is that your young gentleman?

Beatrice   Indeed. The man I will marry.

Pantaloon   I'd be delighted to be aquainted.

Beatrice   Show him in.

Truffaldino (*to* **Smeraldina**)   Hello again.

Smeraldina (*to* **Truffaldino**)   Hello there.

Truffaldino (*to* **Smeraldina**)   Let's keep this till later, eh?

Smeraldina   What for?

Truffaldino   Nothing. Just you be patient.

Smeraldina (*to* **Truffaldino**)   Patient! Hang on a minute, (*To* **Clarice**.) Madam. May I ask of you a little favour?

Truffaldino *goes out.*

Clarice   What on earth is it now?

Smeraldina (*to* **Clarice**)   Mr Beatrice's servant has proposed to me and I thought maybe you could have a quiet little word with his mistress and get her to give it the OK and I'd be made for life, Miss.

Clarice   Oh, all right, if I get the chance.

Pantaloon   What's going on here?

Clarice   Nothing, sir. Women's business.

Silvio (*aside to* **Clarice**)   Go on, let me in on it.

Clarice (*to* **Silvio**)   Buzz off. It's a secret.

Enter **Florindo** *with* **Truffaldino**.

Florindo   Ladies and gentlemen. Your most humble servant. Are you the master of this house, sir?

Pantaloon   Yours to command.

Florindo   No, allow me the honour, sir. I present myself at Beatrice's instigation. I am sure you are acquainted with our various travails.

Pantaloon   But I have to say, I am delighted it's all worked out in the end.

Silvio   Do you remember me, sir?

Florindo   Indeed I do. You provoked me to a duel.

Silvio   Well, I got my come-uppance. This is the opponent (**Beatrice**) who disarmed me and could have easily taken my life.

Beatrice   But gave it you instead.

Silvio   True.

Clarice   Only because I pleaded for you.

Pantaloon   All's well that ends well, eh.

Truffaldino (*to* **Florindo**)   Mr Florindo, sir. Don't forget that word, I mentioned.

Florindo   What word?

Truffaldino   The word, sir. What you promised.

Florindo   I don't remember promising you anything.

Truffaldino   But, sir, to ask Mr Pantaloon for the girl.

Florindo   Oh, all right then. Mr Pantaloon, I really shouldn't be troubling you right now with this . . .

Pantaloon   Please, go right ahead.

Florindo   My servant wishes to marry your maid. Any objections?

Smeraldina (*aside*)   Bloody hell, another one! It's my lucky day!

Pantaloon   Can't see why not. If he's decent and honest man. What do you say?

Smeraldina   Well, it depends on what he looks like, doesn't it. A girl in my position has to be choosy.

Florindo   For the short time I've known him he has been a beacon of trustworthiness and intelligence.

Clarice   Mr Florindo, I'm afraid you have anticipated me in something I was going to do. You see, I was about to speak for my maid and ask Miss Beatrice if Smeraldina could have permission to marry his servant.

Florindo   Well, in that case I must immediately withdraw my request and leave it up to the good lady in question.

Clarice   But I could never put my interests above yours, sir.

Florindo   Consider the matter closed. I refuse to let him marry her.

Clarice   Well, rather than slight you, sir, neither man shall have her.

Truffaldino   Fantastic. Falling over themselves to do me out of a wife.

Smeraldina   One minute I've got two. The next minute I've got bugger-all.

Pantaloon   For God's sake, if the poor lass wants a husband, at least let her have one or the other.

Truffaldino   Excuse me. If I could be so bold. Mr Florindo, have you or have you not asked that Smeraldina marry your servant?

Florindo   You heard me ask yourself. Did you not?

Truffaldino   And Miss Clarice, were you or were you not intending Smeraldina to marry Miss Beatrice's manservant?

Clarice   That's what I intended.

Truffaldino   In that case give me your hand.

Pantaloon   Hang on a minute.

Truffaldino   You see, I am servant to both Florindo and Miss Beatrice.

Florindo   I beg your pardon.

Beatrice   What exactly are you saying?

Truffaldino   Everybody stay calm. Mr Florindo, sir. Who asked you to ask Mr Pantaloon for Smeraldina?

Florindo   You.

Truffaldino   And Miss Clarice, who was it you thought Smeraldina wanted to marry?

Clarice   Well, you.

Truffaldino   Therefore, ipto fatso, Smeraldina is mine.

Florindo   But Beatrice, where is your servant?

Beatrice   Here. Truffaldino.

Florindo   Truffaldino is my servant.

Beatrice   But isn't your servant Pasqual?

Florindo   No, Pasqual is your servant.

Beatrice   What?

Florindo   You deceiful little arse.

Truffaldino   But, sir, don't you see, this is a miracle of time management, sir, a thing to be applauded not condemned. There was nothing except a good honest day's graft and had I not fell in love, sir, you would never have known at all. It's all right for you running round with your banker's bonds and your fancy costumes. We've got to fit our love life in between forty years' hard labour. Look, I didn't mean any harm. I've served you both and give or take a few complications when you might have killed yourself and that, it's worked out pretty well, I mean everybody's happy, aren't they.
All I ask now is :
you forgive the faults of my performance what I didn't get right,
so I can serve Smeraldina, and bid you all good night.

A SELECTED LIST OF
METHUEN MODERN PLAYS

☐ CLOSER	Patrick Marber	£6.99
☐ THE BEAUTY QUEEN OF LEENANE	Martin McDonagh	£6.99
☐ A SKULL IN CONNEMARA	Martin McDonagh	£6.99
☐ THE LONESOME WEST	Martin McDonagh	£6.99
☐ THE CRIPPLE OF INISHMAAN	Martin McDonagh	£6.99
☐ THE STEWARD OF CHRISTENDOM	Sebastian Barry	£6.99
☐ SHOPPING AND F***ING	Mark Ravenhill	£6.99
☐ FAUST (FAUST IS DEAD)	Mark Ravenhill	£5.99
☐ COPENHAGEN	Michael Frayn	£6.99
☐ POLYGRAPH	Robert Lepage and Marie Brassard	£6.99
☐ BEAUTIFUL THING	Jonathan Harvey	£6.99
☐ MEMORY OF WATER & FIVE KINDS OF SILENCE	Shelagh Stephenson	£7.99
☐ WISHBONES	Lucinda Coxon	£6.99
☐ BONDAGERS & THE STRAW CHAIR	Sue Glover	£9.99
☐ SOME VOICES & PALE HORSE	Joe Penhall	£7.99
☐ KNIVES IN HENS	David Harrower	£6.99
☐ BOYS' LIFE & SEARCH AND DESTROY	Howard Korder	£8.99
☐ THE LIGHTS	Howard Korder	£6.99
☐ SERVING IT UP & A WEEK WITH TONY	David Eldridge	£8.99
☐ INSIDE TRADING	Malcolm Bradbury	£6.99
☐ MASTERCLASS	Terrence McNally	£5.99
☐ EUROPE & THE ARCHITECT	David Grieg	£7.99
☐ BLUE MURDER	Peter Nichols	£6.99
☐ BLASTED & PHAEDRA'S LOVE	Sarah Kane	£7.99

• All Methuen Drama books are available through mail order or from your local bookshop.

Please send cheque/eurocheque/postal order (sterling only) Access, Visa, Mastercard, Diners Card, Switch or Amex.

☐☐☐☐☐☐☐☐☐☐☐☐☐☐☐☐

Expiry Date: _____ Signature: _____

Please allow 75 pence per book for post and packing U.K.
Overseas customers please allow £1.00 per copy for post and packing.

ALL ORDERS TO:

Methuen Books, Books by Post, TBS Limited, The Book Service, Colchester Road, Frating Green, Colchester, Essex CO7 7DW.

NAME: _____

ADDRESS: _____

_____

_____

Please allow 28 days for delivery. Please tick box if you do not wish to receive any additional information ☐

Prices and availability subject to change without notice.

METHUEN STUDENT EDITIONS

- All Methuen Drama books are available through mail order or from your local bookshop.

Please send cheque/eurocheque/postal order (sterling only) Access, Visa, Mastercard, Diners Card, Switch or Amex.

☐☐☐☐☐☐☐☐☐☐☐☐☐☐☐☐

Expiry Date:_____ Signature: _____

Please allow 75 pence per book for post and packing U.K.
Overseas customers please allow £1.00 per copy for post and packing.

ALL ORDERS TO:

Methuen Books, Books by Post, TBS Limited, The Book Service, Colchester Road, Frating Green, Colchester, Essex CO7 7DW.

NAME: _____

ADDRESS: _____

_____

Please allow 28 days for delivery. Please tick box if you do not wish to receive any additional information ☐

Prices and availability subject to change without notice.

Companies, institutions and other organisations wishing to make bulk
purchases of any Methuen Drama books should contact their local
bookseller or Methuen direct: Methuen Drama, 215 Vauxhall Bridge
Road, London SW1V 1EJ. Tel: 0171 828 2838; Fax: 0171 828 2098.
For a FREE Methuen Drama catalogue please contact Methuen Drama
at the above address.